"There's a wealth of inspirational stories here...The real charm of the stories in these pages is that they are alive with regular people who just happen to be amazing...BE THE MIRACLE is a book that will give you a boost, teach you how to breathe and open your mind to the miracles happening all around you." —*BookPage*

"Begin the year on a positive note by checking out bestselling author Brett's latest...Read just one of these inspiring (and entertaining) anecdotes of morally heroic everyday people and you'll be tempted to read them all—and then go out and change your corner of the world." —*Family Circle*

Praise for
GOD NEVER BLINKS

"A rousing inspirational collection. Most of her pieces...are short, sweet, and frequently resonant...Complimenting her own experience with anecdotes from friends and others, as well as poems, prayers, psalms, and excerpts from treasured books, Brett employs a veteran writer's knack for keen observation and thorough self-knowledge, delivering hard-earned wisdom with deceptive ease." —*Publishers Weekly*

"Both wise and moving, and a remarkable testimony to the power and love of God." —*BookPage*

"Provide[s] humor, good advice, and an instant mood booster...enough to cover just about any situation you may face in your daily life." —BookLoons.com

"This book is a jewel...sprinkled with life mantras to keep you ticking no matter what situation you face. An amazing book! I surely will be passing this little treasure on." —MomLikeMe.com

"I dare anyone to read this book and keep dry eyes. These essays will speak to your heart and make you rethink your life. This is one of those books, like the original column, that will be shared among friends." —SpiritualWomanThoughts.blogspot.com

"Her book is an anecdotal seminar on keeping life's vicissitudes in their proper perspective." —*Feagler and Friends*, PBS

"Regina Brett is a gifted observer of the experiences that shape who we are, and her lessons unfold with buoyancy, humor, and a courageous honesty. She has given us a beautifully written road map for life." —Jeffrey Zaslow, author of *The Girls from Ames*

"How can one be so lucky as to live in the city where the morning cup of coffee comes with the joy and power of Regina Brett? Her writing entertains as it stimulates change."

—Dr. Michael Roizen, chief wellness officer
for the Cleveland Clinic, and coauthor of
YOU: The Owner's Manual, written
with Dr. Mehmet Oz

"I intend to give my 82-year-old dad a copy of *God Never Blinks*. I will also buy one for a 16-year-old friend. This wise, compassionate, and honest book is a blueprint for living a happy, fulfilling life. Its lessons are timeless—and timely."

—Thrity Umrigar, author of *The Space Between Us*

"A book surely to be received by many a graduate this commencement season."   —Ohio.com

"I love this book! It is powerful, poignant, funny, and magical. Read it and Regina Brett's magic will touch your heart."

—Joe Eszterhas, author of *Crossbearer*
and *Hollywood Animal*

BE
THE
MIRACLE

*50 Lessons for Making
the Impossible Possible*

REGINA BRETT

GRAND CENTRAL
PUBLISHING

New York   Boston

All Scripture quotations are taken from the King James version of the Bible.

Grand Central Publishing
Hachette Book Group
237 Park Avenue
New York, NY 10017

www.HachetteBookGroup.com

Printed in the United States of America

RRD-C

Originally published in hardcover by Grand Central Publishing.

First trade edition: January 2013

10 9 8 7 6 5 4 3 2 1

Grateful acknowledgment is made to quote from the following:

Columns that originally appeared in the *Plain Dealer* are reprinted with permission of the Plain Dealer Publishing Co. The *Plain Dealer* holds the copyright for columns written by Regina Brett from 2000 to 2011. All rights reserved.

Columns that originally appeared in the *Beacon Journal* are reprinted with permission of the Beacon Journal Publishing Co. Inc. The *Beacon Journal* holds the copyright for columns written by Regina Brett from 1994 to 2000. All rights reserved.

Grand Central Publishing is a division of Hachette Book Group, Inc.
The Grand Central Publishing name and logo is a trademark of Hachette Book Group, Inc.

The Hachette Speakers Bureau provides a wide range of authors for speaking events. To find out more, go to www.hachettespeakersbureau.com or call (866) 376-6591.

The publisher is not responsible for websites (or their content) that are not owned by the publisher.

The Library of Congress has cataloged the hardcover edition as follows:
Brett, Regina.
    Be the miracle : 50 lessons for making the impossible possible / Regina Brett. — 1st ed.
        p. cm.
    ISBN 978-1-4555-0033-8
    1. Kindness.   2. Possibility.   3. Miracles.   I. Title.
    BJ1533.K5B74 2012
    158—dc22   2011011098

ISBN 978-1-4555-0032-1 (pbk.)

To Gabrielle,

my first miracle

Contents

Introduction

We all pass by miracle workers every day.

Most of the time they're disguised as ordinary folks, teachers, hairdressers, nurses, secretaries, cashiers, cabdrivers, and the like.

I've never forgotten the day I was a ball of stress and stopped to pay for parking at an outdoor lot. In most parking lots, you pull up, the person sticks his or her hand out of a little booth, takes your money, gives you change, and you pull away. Your eyes never meet and neither of you remembers the encounter.

This time the attendant stood tall, popped his head out, and gave me the biggest smile. He looked me in the eye, greeted me, shook my hand, and gave me a blessing before I left.

He told me he loved his job and saw it as his ministry to bless people as they passed through his parking lot into the rest of their day. Where I saw a mere money collector, he saw a mission in life. He left me feeling renewed and calm.

We've all had moments like that. They happen when you are with people who know that everyone matters, that you don't have to make a lot of money to make a big difference, that you can simply start where you are and magnify the good.

It's so easy to feel overwhelmed by all the problems in the world. How many times have you heard someone say, "Why doesn't someone do something about that?" Or the words come out of your own mouth, as they have mine. We hear about bad news and whisper, "It'll take a miracle to fix that." And we wait and wait and wait for someone else to be the miracle.

We want someone else to act. But miracles aren't what other people do. They're what each of us does. They're what happens when ordinary people take extraordinary action. To be a miracle doesn't mean you have to tackle problems across the globe. It means making a difference in your own living room, cubicle, neighborhood, community.

For the past 26 years, I've had the privilege to be a columnist at the *Plain Dealer* in Cleveland, and before that, work as a journalist at the *Beacon Journal* in Akron. I've had a front-row seat on life. Ordinary people from all walks of life have opened their hearts and shared with me how they've made the impossible possible. You'll meet some of them in this book, since some of these essays originally appeared in those newspapers.

My cancer journey inspired my first book, *God Never Blinks: 50 Lessons for Life's Little Detours*. I wrote my first 50 lessons in gratitude for being alive to see my odometer turn over to 50. When I was bald from chemotherapy and weak from radiation 13 years ago, I wasn't sure if I would get to grow old. Along the way, I met countless cancer survivors who taught me to get busy on the possible, regardless of the prognosis.

Those 50 lessons traveled the world, first as a column, then as an e-mail forwarded around the country and the world, then as a book. CEOs, pastors, judges, and social workers quote them. They've been reprinted in hundreds of newsletters, church bulletins, and small-town newspapers. People carry the list of lessons in their wallets, pin them to work cubicles, and stick them under refrigerator magnets.

I once heard it said that people read to know they are not alone. I hope these new essays, stories, and columns reflect personal truths that are universal to all. I hope this book will both help you embrace yourself as is and challenge you to be your best self to go make something possible.

We can't do everything, and what we can do, we can't do perfectly, but that's okay. All we need to do is make a beginning, right here, right now. If we just do that, it will make all the difference in the world.

The
Fifty
Lessons

Start where you are.

There's an old saying: "If you think you're too small to make a difference, you've never been in a tent with a mosquito."

Every time I hear that, my ears cringe at the thought of the power that one pesky little bug has to keep me up all night and itching all day. The truth is, we're all big or small enough or whatever size necessary to make a difference.

When I was a newspaper reporter in Akron, Ohio, I was once assigned to cover a breaking news story about a little girl who had been kidnapped one day in September. Jessica Repp was just nine years old that Monday afternoon when she left home on her pink bicycle. When she was two blocks from home, a man drove up and asked her if she knew someone in the neighborhood. Then he got out of his car, opened his trunk, and pretended to get something. Suddenly, he grabbed Jessica off the sidewalk, threw her into the trunk of his car, and sped away.

Jessica's dad called the *Beacon Journal* newsroom begging us to write a story about his missing daughter. His call came late in the day, leaving little time to write anything beyond the few facts he knew and a general description of the girl. The police hadn't yet confirmed any of the investigation details because it was all so fresh. There weren't a lot of facts available. This was before Amber Alerts and 24/7 news on endless cable channels. One of our reporters, Sheryl Harris, stayed late at work that day to gather every scrap of detail she could from the dad. She made the extra effort to be sure we carried the girl's photo in the next day's paper. Sheryl barely had time to write anything beyond a description of the girl with the blonde hair and the pink T-shirt.

Jessica was still missing 24 hours later. By then the news had spread all over the media. I stood outside her home with a horde of reporters as we waited for the bad news that would surely come. Any law enforcement officer will tell you, once a child is missing 24 hours, that child isn't coming back. Ministers poured in and out of the home along with neighbors and church people. It already looked like a funeral.

Can you imagine being the parent of a missing child? Praying and sitting by the phone all night, hoping each call will bring news of a miracle. Instead, Jessica's mom, dad, sister, and brother awoke to police helicopters searching for her body; mounted deputies combing the nearby cornfields for her remains; the sheriff, FBI agents, and dozens of police scattered everywhere in their neighborhood. Deputies even took a boat to search nearby lakes. Police dogs sniffed Jessica's favorite teddy bear and were out tracking the scent of the missing girl.

A lone boy walked up and down the street, pacing back and forth to and from the sheriff's cruiser parked out front. Jessica's brother, Jonathan, was 13. He kept asking whether his sister had been found. His eyes were bloodshot from crying, from waking up all night to check her bed, praying he'd find her safe and asleep in it.

As I watched the police efforts above and around me, I prayed for her and her family. I was standing on the sidewalk outside her home when all of a sudden it seemed as though the entire house screamed.

The police had found Jessica.

Alive.

Her mom, sister, brother, and everyone burst from the home, weeping and praising God. Her dad had been running off more copies of her picture when he got word. He left the copies and ran to the hospital.

The reporters all raced to the hospital. Police there wouldn't say what had happened to the girl. When they had asked her for details, she wept.

It turned out that at 5 a.m. the kidnapper brought the girl into a Dairy Mart in Barberton. A convenience store clerk—one of those lowliest of workers on life's career ladder—had been diligently waiting on customers when a man walked into the store with a little girl who looked terrified. The clerk stared at the girl then stared at the photo of Jessica Repp in the newspaper article that Sheryl wrote. It matched. The clerk called the police.

That convenience store clerk saved the girl's life. The clerk identified the kidnapper, who had been there before as a customer. A while later, a clerk at a gas station called police after a man came in acting strange. The store videotape confirmed it was the kidnapper. He had stopped to buy cigarettes. Just before 11 a.m., police spotted his car in a parking lot. The little girl was sitting next to the man.

Police said the man involved had a history of untreated mental illness and erratic behavior. Officers said he most likely would have soon panicked and killed the girl.

My friend Sheryl went on to win a Pulitzer Prize—the biggest award a journalist can win—years later for her work on a big series the newspaper wrote about race relations. Sheryl doesn't even remember writing that small story on Jessica Repp. It was too small to make a difference in her career. It wasn't award-winning journalism, but I always think of it as something better. It was lifesaving journalism.

The most important story she ever wrote was probably one of the smallest. It might not have even carried her name, I don't recall. But it helped save a child's life.

I never knew what happened to the gas station attendant or the convenience store worker who was the first to report seeing the girl and the kidnapper. So often those workers are anonymous people we don't even look in the eye when we buy a gallon of milk, a pack of cigarettes, or a tank of gas.

But that story changed the way I see those we pass by every day who work in jobs most of us wouldn't want. Those workers taught me that no one is unimportant or too small to make a difference.

If you want to change the world in a big way, you do your small assignments with greater love, greater attention, greater passion. Simply embrace the job you have, the family you have, the neighborhood you have, the task you have been given.

You never know what can happen when you simply act on the possibilities right in front of you. When you start where you are, you could simply ring up milk, cigarettes, and gas. Or you might just save a life.

Get busy on the possible.

The impossible can start with something as small as a lump.

For years I heeded the warning: Do monthly breast self-exams. Like most women, I did them on a "sort of" basis. Every few months I'd sort of do a quick feel, but never as thoroughly as the doctors urged. I didn't want to go looking for trouble. If you look for it, you might find it. Looking for cancer is unsettling. Thank God I looked.

One night when I ran the pads of my fingers in a circle around my breast, my fingers came to a halt. How long had that hard spot been here? It was probably nothing, but it wasn't there the last time I checked. That nothing turned out to be stage II breast cancer. A surgeon removed a tumor the size of a grape.

When you hear the word *cancer,* it's as if someone took the game of life and tossed it in the air. All the pieces go flying.

The pieces land on a new board. Everything has shifted. You don't know where to start. The fear subsides once you can actually take action, once you get busy on the possible.

Before I started chemotherapy treatments, I wrote down the best advice from doctors, family, friends, books, and survivors and created an Owner's Manual to help me take care of myself. It would remind me that cancer is doable. I made a plan to get through four months of chemotherapy and six weeks of daily radiation. My manual began with a vow to survive:

I, Regina, vow to get well. I vow to participate in my treatment, even if it means enduring temporary physical, emotional, and mental changes in my life. I vow to stick with this course of treatment and not look back. I vow to do everything in my power to heal and to live.

When you have cancer, it's like you enter a new time zone: the Cancer Zone. Everything in the Tropic of Cancer revolves around your health or your sickness. I didn't want my whole life to revolve around cancer. Life came first; cancer came second. So I came up with a game plan: Celebrate life in the midst of cancer. Enjoy time with all the people I love, read all the books on my to-read list, watch all the movies I had missed, and buy the piano I always wanted. My plan was to keep as much of my life intact as possible: write my newspaper column, play volleyball, teach my college writing class.

On the morning of the first chemotherapy appointment, I filled my backpack with a water bottle, my Owner's Manual, a notepad, pens, hard candy, a CD player, CDs, headphones, and books. The appointment would last only an hour or two, but I was ready for anything. I sank into the recliner as if it were a beach chair, adjusted the headphones, and listened to Louis Armstrong sing, "I see trees of green, red roses, too, I see them bloom, for me and you. And I think to myself, what a wonderful world."

And it was a wonderful world, even though it seemed to revolve around cancer for a year. When I got breast cancer in 1998, there was nowhere in the area to go for support groups that didn't require money or insurance. Each hospital had its own program, but there was no central place to be with other survivors and try yoga, massage, Reiki, exercise, journaling, and other holistic healing aids.

A year into my recovery, Eileen Saffran showed up in my life. She had a dream. Eileen wanted to create a place where anyone touched by cancer could come and get every bit of support she or he needed for free. I sat at the table with dozens she invited to that first planning meeting. Her dream seemed too big, too vast, too impossible. I doubted it could ever become a reality, so I bowed out. I was still weak from radiation and the lingering effects of chemo brain and couldn't imagine how her plan could ever get off the ground.

Eileen was a clinical social worker whose parents were diagnosed with cancer within six months of each other. Her dad had lung cancer; her mother had non-Hodgkin's lymphoma. Her parents died within three years of each other. Being with them through their treatments made her realize people needed a place to go for help. Eileen envisioned a center that didn't smell, feel, and look like a hospital. A place where people didn't need the right insurance to get counseling. A place where people didn't need a referral from a doctor for a massage. A place where anyone touched by cancer could get free support services. A place where people didn't feel so alone.

Eileen worked with oncology and psychology patients. She assembled an advisory board, met with cancer experts and organizations. She researched wellness centers all over the country. She launched the website touchedbycancer.org. She opened the doors to The Gathering Place 18 months after that first meeting. I never figured out how she got it up and running. How did she do it?

"Optimistic naïveté," she confided.

When I visit The Gathering Place I think of that line from Alice in Wonderland when the young girl says, "There is no use trying; one can't believe impossible things," to which the White Queen replies, "I daresay you haven't had much practice. When I was your age, I always did it for half an hour a day. Why, sometimes I've believed as many as six impossible things before breakfast."

If you want to accomplish the impossible, get busy on the possible.

Eileen created the Switzerland of health care. It's a stand-alone, independent, community cancer center. There are no territorial battles between hospitals. It doesn't matter where anyone got medical treatment. All are welcome. Every service is free to anyone touched by cancer. The center offers massage, hands-on healing, journaling, tai chi, yoga, nutrition programs, exercise, and support groups for nearly every type of cancer. There are support groups on how to move forward, look better, find inner peace, and programs on forgiveness, pampering, and healthy cooking. A medical librarian provides consultations on medical bills, clinical trials, and cancer treatments. Volunteer attorneys write living wills and help with estate planning.

It's a place of healing and hope. A place where you are never asked to pull out your insurance card. A place that doesn't feel like an institution. There are no shots, no blood draws, no medical treatments or tests. It's more like a home with a fireplace, original art hanging on the walls, and cozy furniture. Everything has been donated by individuals or organizations.

The Gathering Place started in a storefront in 2000 with 6,100 square feet. It doubled its space and went from an annual operating budget of $360,000 a year to $1.8 million. The building is already paid for. The place runs solely on contributions from individuals and organizations and with the help of 350 volunteers.

Where there was once a pile of dirt, a healing garden flourishes with fountains and waterfalls, stone carvings and bird feeders. Iron gates depict, intricate labyrinths. A storybook maze about transformation leads through a metal caterpillar cocoon to a giant silver butterfly. It's a place that reminds you it's a wonderful world, even if you're fighting cancer or helping someone you love face it.

We don't yet have a cure for cancer, but people like Eileen cure the fear of cancer by offering hope. So can the rest of us. We do it by getting busy on the possible, no matter how impossible it seems.

You can make a big difference, no matter how little you make.

As a journalist, I've been branded Sally Social Worker for trying to help people too much. It's no insult to be called a bleeding heart when I think of all the things social workers do to stanch the bleeding, to help the lost, the lonely, the forgotten.

A few years ago when I was asked to give the commencement address at the Mandel School of Applied Social Sciences at Case Western Reserve University, I wasn't sure what message to give. Before addressing the graduates, I asked all my friends who are social workers what I should say. They told me to be funny. Social workers could use a good laugh. Tell jokes, they said.

Jokes? I didn't know any jokes about social work, except the ones my friends sent me:

How many social workers does it take to change a lightbulb?
None. They empower the bulb to change itself.

How many social workers does it take to change a lightbulb?
None. The bulb isn't burned out, it's just differently lit.

How many social workers does it take to change a lightbulb?
None. They set up a team to write a paper on coping with darkness.

And my favorite:

How many social workers does it take to change a lightbulb?
The lightbulb doesn't need changing. It's the system that needs to change.

They also told me the old story about the mugger with a gun who confronts a social worker. The mugger yells, "Your money or your life!" "I'm sorry," the social worker answers, "I'm a social worker, so I have no money . . . and no life."

The same could be said of police officers, nurses, teachers, and so many others who are on the front lines of life. They matter so much, yet often make so little. Last time I checked, the starting pay for social workers hovered around $28,000.

No, they don't make much. Or do they?

The poet Taylor Mali changed my mind. His powerful words about what teachers make have been forwarded all over the world in e-mails. He inspired me to rethink what social workers make.

Teachers don't get paid what they are worth. They don't

sit around boasting about their salaries and summer homes and vacations in the South of France. The paycheck and perks are probably pathetic compared to the endless hours and passion put into planning lessons, grading papers, counseling students, and pulling parents off the ceiling.

Mali summed up how teachers matter by making children work harder than anyone ever imagined possible. Teachers can make earning a C+ comparable to winning a Medal of Honor if a child did his best. They can also make getting an A– feel like getting an F if the child could have done better. Teachers have the power to make parents tremble in fear at a teacher conference and follow-up calls home.

Mali made me think of Mr. Ricco, my ninth-grade English teacher. He could have been anything. He could have gone anywhere. He loved opera, poetry, and fine wine. But there he was, teaching surly ninth graders at Brown Junior High in Ravenna, Ohio, how to write one good, decent paragraph.

There was Mr. Maske, the high school choir teacher. When I sing in the shower, sometimes it's the alto part to the score of *West Side Story* he taught me. I envied the sopranos their melodies, but he taught me that all the parts matter—even the small ones. I didn't believe him until we piled onto those bleachers in the school auditorium. Damn if we didn't sound almost like the Mormon Tabernacle Choir. Every time I hear "The Battle Hymn of the Republic," I see his hands dancing in the air, blending our wobbly voices into one beautiful song.

Then there was Mr. Roberto, who told me at least once a week, "There's no such thing as a free lunch, Brett." That science teacher used your last name as if it were the period to every sentence. He was our own personal Marine Corps drill sergeant. He's the reason I recycle. The reason I pick up rocks in a creek to see what's crawling underneath. The reason I snip the tops off plants to make them grow bushier. The reason I wanted to be a forest ranger.

There are so many more teachers whose names faded but whose imprint never will. Because of a teacher, I can balance a checkbook, figure compound interest, and calculate how much paint covers a 10-by-16-foot room. Because of a teacher, I absolutely LOVE to read, and when you love to read, the whole world opens up.

So many people do that in their occupations. They open up the world. Unfortunately, too many of them are at the bottom of the pay scale. Which brings me back to the lowly social worker.

Social workers, like most teachers, don't make much. Or do they?

What do they make?

They make an infertile couple celebrate a lifetime of Mother's Days and Father's Days by helping them adopt a crack baby no one else wants.

They make a child fall asleep every night without fear of his father's fists.

They make a homeless veteran feel at home in the world.

They make a teenager decide to stop cutting herself.

They make a beaten woman find the courage to leave her abuser for good.

They make a boy with Down syndrome feel like the smartest kid on the bus.

What do they make?

They make a ten-year-old believe that he is loved and

wanted, regardless of how long he lasts in the next foster home.

They make a teen father count to ten and leave the room so he won't shake his newborn son.

They make a man with schizophrenia see past his demons.

They make a rape victim talk about it for the first time in years.

They make an ex-convict put down the bottle and hold down a job.

What do they make?

They make a couple communicate so well they decide not to get divorced.

They make a dying cancer patient make peace with her past, with her brief future, with her God.

They make the old man whose wife has Alzheimer's cherish the good times, when she still remembered him.

They make forgotten people feel cherished, not-so-beautiful people feel beautiful, confused people feel understood, broken people feel whole.

What do they make?

As Mali said about teachers, they make more than most people will ever make.

They make a difference.

Magnify the good.

They carry the labels the world gives them—bum, loser, ex-con, alcoholic, prostitute—until they meet Larry Petrus and discover those labels are all wrong.

Few people who walk through the doors of the West Side Catholic Center in Cleveland make a good impression. They lead with their anger. They mumble requests for money. They smell of last night's Wild Irish Rose. They wear clothes that haven't been washed in weeks.

Larry, who was 76 when I met him, didn't see any of that when he volunteered at the Cleveland agency on Tuesday and Thursday mornings. Larry doesn't have 20/20 vision when it comes to the poor. He doesn't see the grime, the failure, the shame.

He slides a pair of bifocals over sea-gray eyes and there he is, face-to-face with God's own sons and daughters.

"I go from what God thinks of them," he said. "God does not regret any of His creations."

When he started volunteering more than ten years ago, he sorted clothes. Then one day someone asked for help writing a résumé. Pretty soon everyone was asking him to write them. They started calling him the Résumé Man. They hung up a sign urging people to see Larry if they needed a résumé.

"The résumé is like a label on a can. It tells a person what they are, what they got inside of them, what they have to offer," Larry said in a voice so soft I had to lean in to hear him.

The man with the baby-fine white hair and black eyebrows that hang like thick question marks doesn't sit down to collect a history of jobs held and dates worked. He digs deeper, asking, "What did you accomplish there? What are your dreams? Your hopes? Your hobbies?

"There's always something hidden in their lives no one has ever asked," he said.

Larry never delves into why or how they ended up poor. "Society makes them feel guilty enough," he said. He listens as reverently as a priest to anything they feel the need to confess and offers absolution in every hug.

He leaned in and rested his elbows on faded blue jeans to whisper about the woman who had been drinking since she was a child, but is now married and sober. "You wouldn't believe the stories," he said, "the life of prostitution, incest, beatings. You see them with black eyes and broken jaws."

Larry doesn't give up on anybody. "As long as they're alive, there's always hope," he believes.

He tells each of them what a good person they are, tells them to be who God thinks they are. He collects the pieces of themselves that they've lost. One man who was 45 had held only menial jobs, cleaning the Cleveland Indians ball field and working as a dishwasher and a busboy. Larry found out he'd attended college and had wanted to be a teacher. Larry typed under Personal Objective, "I would like to continue college work and pursue a teaching career."

Larry discovered one man had volunteered at a hunger center, so that went on the résumé. Another man worked for a cleaning outfit and supervised ten employees. Larry taught him to say, "I was responsible for . . ." not just, "I worked for . . ."

Larry doesn't merely write down that someone was a punch press operator. He mentions he did 500 parts per hour, that the press weighed 600 tons, that he worked 12-hour shifts. "All these skills!" Larry says, excited over each bit of gold he finds in every prospect.

A retired salesman for a nut and bolt company, Larry types up his notes at home, runs off copies of the résumés, and presents them in a nice folder. When he's done, his paycheck is the look on a face that says, "Wow. I really am something. I do have something to offer."

"I get them to dream of what they can be, to not just be satisfied with where they are. I try to leave them with hope," he said. "And it's free."

He finds the hidden worth in every lost soul who walks in the door because he's trained himself to see it. When you look for the good in everyone, you not only find the good, you magnify it. He reminded me of that line in the Bible, the response Mary gave when she learned she was pregnant. "My soul doth magnify the Lord," Mary says.

My soul has a bad habit of magnifying what isn't so good and godly. Too often I focus my inner magnifying glass on the nasty comment some stranger made, and it grows. Or I put it on the past, on a teacher who made fun of me in third grade, on friends who disappointed me in high school, and the wounds grow deeper. Or I put it on the future, and the endless stream of fear, anxiety, and worry expands into a river that sweeps me away.

What would it mean to have your soul really magnify God? If you saw the good in everyone, the God in everyone, like Larry does?

It would mean that every minute of every day you walked around with a special magnifying glass. In everything you trained it on, you saw God.

Imagine seeing God in your boss. In the woman in the next cubicle. In the driver in front of you on the freeway. In the neighbor who doesn't mow his lawn. In the loud guy on the subway selling candy bars.

Imagine seeing only the good in your spouse. In the husband who snores too loudly and doesn't put down the toilet seat. In the wife who nags too often and never stops talking long enough to listen.

Imagine seeing only good in your children. In the toddler who throws a tantrum in the cookie aisle. In the ten-year-old who refuses to clean her room. In the teenager who wrecks the car he never asked to borrow.

Imagine seeing God in the cancer verdict you just got. Or

in the layoff notice. Or in the pregnancy test that came back positive . . . or negative.

What if you focused your magnifying glass on the good in everything that looks and feels dead in your life, in the marriage you want to give up on, in the job that bores you, in the family that frustrates you, in the person in the mirror?

Whatever I see through that magnifying glass grows bigger.

It's up to me to decide where to aim the lens.

Do your best and forget the rest.
It could simply be too soon to tell.

The worst newspaper column I ever wrote turned out to be one of my best, thanks to a teacher.

Jo Anne Hollis was named Best Educator of the Year at the local vocational school in the town where I grew up. She loved to teach home economics to the learning disabled and students with multiple handicaps. She saw the promise in them that everyone else missed. Her specialty was to make people feel important. Jo Anne was dying of cancer when I interviewed her a few days before Easter for a column that would run on Easter Sunday.

The day after I met her, I wrote a column for that Thursday that turned out to be the worst column I had ever written. I tried to be funny and failed. It was the best I could do on a day when my muse went AWOL.

I wrote an entire column calling Easter the grossest holiday on the calendar. Here's part of the column that ran with the headline "Easter Treats Can Make You a Basket Case":

From a dye-it-eerie point of view, it's enough to make the Easter bunny barf. Every candy maker thinks consumers buy sweets on the basis of color—the brighter, the better. Pepto-Bismol pink is still the No. 1 shade, with Vile Violet a close second.

And why does everything have to come shaped like an egg? Who decided this? Surely not the Easter bunny. Left to their own devices, eggs are downright nasty. The only good egg is a deviled egg.

Robin's-egg-blue candy eggs? They've been around forever, but what kind of kid would want to eat a robin's egg? And just what kind of parent would let him?

Chocolate bunnies are still best sellers, but good luck finding one that doesn't taste like it came from a wax museum. If you think I'm the only one fed up with the candy situation, just wait till Sunday. Don't be surprised if the Easter bunny leaves some little brown droppings by your basket. And they won't be Raisinettes.

My colleagues in the newsroom rolled their eyes when they read it. I overheard one of them say that I must have been running on fumes when I wrote it. A few readers called to criticize it. I felt embarrassed. I had done the best I could with what I had that day, but their criticism hit my INTERNAL DOUBT button, the one that plays the same recording: "What the hell is wrong with you? Can't you do anything right?" The voice of my dad at his worst still plays on inside me on those days when I judge myself too harshly or someone else does.

That voice wore me down until the day I spoke to Jo Anne's husband after my column about her ran on Easter Sunday. I wrote about how the teachers from Maplewood Joint Vocational School in my old hometown, Ravenna, had given her the Best Educator of the Year award.

Jo Anne was 44 and dying of uterine cancer. In just five months it had spread to her colon, liver, lungs, spine, and brain. It was almost harder for her to learn that she wouldn't return to her classroom than to hear that the cancer had spread.

Jo Anne no longer had a classroom but still had lessons to offer from the hospital bed in her home. The first thing she taught me was to look into a person's eyes and call him or her by name. Once her hazel eyes caught mine, they wouldn't let go.

When I interviewed her, she was bedridden, her bald head wrapped in a lovely silk scarf. She beckoned me to come closer so she could look into my eyes as we talked. She exuded a warmth I'd never felt from anyone before or since. It was as if her whole body radiated a light that you couldn't see but you could feel. I felt like I was in the presence of pure love and grace. The closer you got to her, the less you noticed her hair had fallen out, that her skin was growing transparent.

She told me busloads of teachers had shown up in her yard with signs proclaiming WAY TO GO, JO, WORLD-CLASS TEACHER, and TEACHERS TOUCH LIVES. Each one walked across the lawn and stepped up to her bedroom window to thank her. Jo Anne spoke in the present tense about her job even though she knew she'd never go back. Hard coughs punctuated each sentence. She told me why she loved to teach handicapped students.

"When they come into your classroom they look at the floor," she said. "They don't have any self-esteem. They don't have the idea that they are good people. People have put them down. People have shoved them in corners. People have shunned them. One of the greatest gratifications for me is to watch those eyes come off the floor and meet mine and you know they're going to make it."

Her job was to place students in service jobs.

"They can learn job skills anyplace if people have patience with them," she said. "It's a little tougher to learn the life skills."

When she took a vanload of students to get fast food, she stopped at each child's favorite restaurant to let them exert their individual choices. At the United Church of Christ where she was a Sunday school teacher, she started the Intentional Care Unit where members visited the sick, sent cards, and offered rides to the hospital.

As a Girl Scout leader, she put fun first. Her Scouts didn't always rough it when camping.

"Once a year we go to the Sheraton," she confided, whispering like a child passing along a secret. "If the girls want to spend their cookie money there, that's fine with me. I just like to have fun. You make it fun and they'll remember it for the rest of their lives, whether it's schoolwork, housework, or church work."

The most important job she worried about leaving was motherhood. She wanted to live long enough to see her son, Tony, who was 16, become an Eagle Scout, and her daughter,

Dawn, who was 14, be confirmed in the church. She knew she wouldn't live to see them graduate or marry or have children. She wanted them to remember how much she loved them. She wanted them to know that the beauty and wonder of each day were theirs to celebrate simply by waking to it. Jo Anne loved the dawn.

"Oh, it's beautiful. You see that sunrise start to come up and you know that's the glory of God," she said in a voice that was fading fast.

She wanted her children and her students to share her life's job description, which she found in her favorite book of the Bible, Ephesians: "Walk worthy of the vocation wherewith ye are called, with all lowliness and meekness, with long-suffering, forbearing one another in love . . . Now are ye light in the Lord: walk as children of light."

Her light went out on Easter Sunday. Jo Anne Hollis died at dawn, her favorite time of day.

When I heard that she had died, I called her husband, Bill.

"You know that column you wrote about Easter candy?" he asked.

I braced myself. *Oh, no,* I thought. *Did it push her over the edge? Was it that bad?*

He wanted me to know that he had sat next to her hospital bed and read it to her.

"She laughed and laughed," he told me. "Later that afternoon, she slipped into a coma. She never woke up. I want to thank you for that column. It was the last time we ever laughed together."

That was Jo Anne's gift to me. To know that even at my worst, I can still be a gift. To know that even meager efforts can touch one person in a profound way. To know that the results of what I do are none of my business.

I think of Jo Anne Hollis every time I judge myself or someone else too harshly. How do we really know the worth of our work? It's not our job to judge the worth of what we offer the world, but to keep offering it regardless.

You might never know the true worth of your efforts. Or it could simply be too soon to tell.

We all do the same things. It's how we do them that makes the difference.

Everyone brought a gift for the wedding shower, but one stood out. It was so lovely, the bride-to-be didn't want to unwrap it. The box was wrapped in a silvery white paper and tied with gold, green, and burgundy ribbon and had a cluster of the most real-looking grapes spilling out from the center. It was absolutely stunning. It looked more like a centerpiece for the wedding table than a gift for a shower.

We all oohed and aahed, gushing over the package, wondering out loud what store had done such an incredible job of gift wrapping. It turned out that the woman sitting next to me had wrapped it herself. I've never forgotten what Sandy Horton said when I complimented her gift.

"Someone taught me long ago, we all do the same things," she told me. "It's how we do them."

I think of that often, especially when I meet people in

average, ordinary jobs who add a flare to make them extraordinary. Anyone who has ever stepped foot into Valerie's Happy Restroom never forgets how she does business.

"Welcome to Valerie's Restroom," she calls out. Her motto is "Don't worry. Pee happy."

My daughter ran into her on a stop at the Charlotte airport in North Carolina. It's Valerie's job to clean the restroom. She never stops smiling or singing.

"You are my sunshine, my only sunshine," she sings to every woman who walks in.

"There are plenty of seats for you. No line, no waiting. No waiting, no line," she says as she dances along, opening stall doors to invite patrons in. "If you can't have fun at work, don't go. It's the VIP. It's very important that you get a seat in Valerie's Happy Restroom. This is where you go to pee happy!"

This is a woman who cleans a public restroom all day long. This is a woman who could see herself on the lowest rung of life's career ladder. Instead, she elevates everyone's spirit, no matter where they stand on the rung of life.

"Gotta go, gotta go, gotta go right now," she sings, and claps gloved hands.

You've got to admire her joy for life in what—pun intended—could be a pretty crappy job.

There are others who bring that kind of joy into their work. I once read an obituary of a nurse who sang to patients. The patients all treasured her songs and asked for the Singing Nurse.

Then there's Robert McIntyre, who works as greeter at the Cleveland Clinic. It's his job to offer a hand, a wheelchair, or directions to patients and their families as they enter and leave the cancer center. Robert does it with flare: he wears a red coat and a black top hat and sings to everyone.

He never aspired to be a singer. He joined the church choir once, but they couldn't rein in Brother McIntyre. He's supposed to be a tenor, but his voice wanders wherever it wants to go.

"I just freelance what sounds good for me in my throat," he said.

His singing career started in a parking garage at another hospital 15 years ago. He was a garage attendant who liked the acoustics of the parking deck. One day he brought a tape recorder, made sure he was alone, then belted out "Under the Boardwalk."

"It was just me and the cars," he said.

When he stopped, he heard thunderous applause. He turned and saw 30 people clapping.

Oops, he thought. *I'm gonna lose my job.*

From that point on, he has been singing every chance he gets. He performs daily at the Cleveland Clinic's Taussig Cancer Center, serenading patients in his red coat and black top hat.

"I'm sort of a concierge, greeter, transport," he said. "I'm a conglomerate of different things."

His name tag shows a bald man under the size 7¾ top hat he saved from his job as a doorman at a fancy hotel. Whenever he doesn't wear it, he calls himself "Undercover Brother." He keeps the hat in a silver cabinet by the information desk with a gallon-size plastic zip bag of laminated family photos. One photo shows his brother, who died from lung cancer.

"I sang for him," he said. "I did the whole works."

Robert's playlist includes "I Can See Clearly Now," "Sweet Hour of Prayer," "You've Lost That Lovin' Feeling," "Mr. Bojangles," and "God Is Still on the Throne." He makes the patients feel like royalty. They arrive weak from cancer or chemo, leaning on canes and walkers. He lifts them with a smile and a song.

After five years here, everyone knows him. During a rendition of "You Are Everything," a woman interrupted. "Are you Robert?" she asked. "I've heard good things about you."

He smiled and asked, "What can I do for you?"

He headed outside to a van, took a thin hand in his, and guided a woman into a wheelchair. Robert doesn't pry, doesn't ask questions. And when he sings, he keeps the volume low. People often ask him, "Where do you sing?"

"Here, right here," he answers.

When they tell him he should be a professional, he tells them, "I am. I'm a professional cancer center singer."

For one patient, he took his singing on the road. Robert always sang "Smoke Gets in Your Eyes" to Shirley Dorsey. Shirley came in for radiation and chemotherapy to fight melanoma. She didn't respond to the chemo, but she did to Robert. He sang her hymns. And when she died, her husband, Ed, asked Robert to sing at the funeral.

Robert wore his red coat and top hat. He sang "Order My Steps." Ed invited him to stay for dinner and meet the whole family. Ed credits Robert for Shirley's last days of life.

"He'd just cheer her up," Ed said. "He probably extended her life."

Robert shakes off the praise.

"I never set out to do this," he said. "It took me years to realize this is my calling."

He turned a job into a calling. We all have that option. We all do the same things; it's how we do them that makes the difference. We become a gift to others when we make them feel they are the gift.

Interruptions are divine assignments.

One day I was on my way to interview someone for a newspaper column and got lost in an unfamiliar part of Cleveland. After driving up and down the block a few times, I stopped in a small ice-cream shop named Scoops. I interrupted the teen behind the counter to ask for directions. He was so helpful, I promised to come back later and get a cone.

When I returned hours later to order ice cream, the teenager scooped my butter-pecan cone with a precision I'd never seen. He even weighed the cone. He was a black inner-city teen, probably 15 or 16, and it was just days before school was to start again for the fall.

As I stood there waiting in silence, I felt the tug at my heart. *Talk to the young man. Step out of your comfort zone.*

"So where are you going to school?" I asked the stranger.

"I don't know," he told me.

One question, and the world opened up.

Terrance Embry told me that he had been going to Hawken School, a prestigious private school in a suburb across town, but his family ran out of money and could no longer afford their small portion of the bill that the scholarship didn't cover.

"What do you want to do?" I asked.

"Oh, I am going to be a neurosurgeon," he told me.

He said it like it was a given, like nothing was going to stop him. Then he spent the next hour telling me exactly how it would happen, regardless of any obstacle.

Terrance wore a white polo shirt, an apron over khakis, and a hat that read SCOOPS, but he acted as if he were already wearing surgical scrubs. Before he prepared each cone, he went to the sink.

Wash. Scrub. Dry. Then scoop.

His smile faded for a brief moment. He told me his mom was looking for work and that his dad was a postal clerk. Terrance had only been working at the ice cream parlor for four weeks.

"If not Hawken, maybe it's not destined," he said, then grinned, as if he knew a secret. "All I see is the outcome—for me to become a neurosurgeon."

He dried his hands then told me how he always wanted to be a doctor. For three summers, he attended an enrichment program to prepare African American boys for sixth, seventh, and eighth grades. There, he read the book *Gifted Hands* by pediatric neurosurgeon Ben Carson. Carson grew up poor, leaning on his mom and his God.

"We had so much in common," Terrance said. "The book was an answer to my prayer. It's like it fell out of the sky."

He didn't get to keep the book.

"But," he said, "I'll remember it vividly for the rest of my life."

Terrance attended Foundation of Truth, a storefront church where he said he had "fun with the Lord." He had taken three years of Latin. He wanted to take Spanish. He pined for advanced biology, chemistry, and physics. He was going to be a junior. He played basketball and ran track.

He was the youngest of seven. One sister was working on her Ph.D. in child psychology. She reminded him daily not to quit.

"I never thought it would be easy. This is just an obstacle. I'm going to go around it," he said, then caught himself. "I'm going to go straight through it."

It wouldn't be easy. His parents split up three years ago.

"Me and my dad used to do everything together," he said. "It kind of tore a hole in our relationship."

And in the family finances.

"We're not poor, but we're not well off," Terrance said.

The previous year, Terrance rode a bus from his West Side home to the private school on the East Side. Most nights he got home at 7 p.m.

"I love Hawken. It's a great school," he said. "They put the responsibility on you."

When he first told people he wanted to be a neurosurgeon, they laughed. Not anymore.

Terrance said he would love to watch a surgery or talk to a neurosurgeon about how the human body works. He still believes he'll graduate from Hawken, then Stanford University, then Columbia.

And from there?

"I'll go anywhere I'm needed," he said.

Then he went back to the sink to prepare for the next customer, who wanted a mint-chocolate-chip cone. Terrance did it with surgical precision.

Wash. Scrub. Dry. Then scoop.

One day it will be wash, scrub, dry, then cut.

When I called Hawken to check out his story, they were stunned that I'd found Terrance. They had been trying to reach him all summer, but the boy's parents hadn't stayed in touch. The school was so glad to find him, they agreed to cover all his expenses.

When the column about him ran, a neurosurgeon's wife read the article and felt a tug. She told her husband about it over lunch. He felt the tug, too. Dr. Mark Luciano saw himself at 16, back when he wanted to study the brain, long before he began operating on it. Dr. Luciano wanted to open the door for Terrance's dream. It's a door that sits past a bright red line painted on the floor at the Cleveland Clinic.

Terrance met Dr. Luciano in a conference room at the hospital. The teen got to put on blue scrubs and a white lab coat. Dr. Luciano sat at the other end and seemed as excited as Terrance was.

"Every new patient is like a puzzle," Dr. Luciano told him. "You have to see if you can solve it."

He operates on babies with fluid in their brains, children with tumors, kids with cranial deformities.

The puzzle on the day they met was a patient with a Chiari decompression. Dr. Luciano used his fist as a brain and ran his finger through it like a spinal cord to show Terrance how the back of the brain was being pressed in by the skull. The cerebellum was being pushed down the hole where the spinal cord comes up.

The doctor was going to let Terrance watch the brain surgery. He warned the teen, some people get nervous, some get nauseated, some last a mere 15 minutes. "If you get sick," he said, "it doesn't mean anything about your future as a doctor."

Terrance sighed and let his shoulders relax.

The doctor explained that the brain feels no pain. He talked about using computer technology to navigate around the brain and joked about how neurosurgeons love gadgets.

Terrance nodded.

They walked down the hall to the operating room. From behind, they looked like two doctors, with Terrance the taller one. Dr. Luciano warned him not to step over the red line painted on the floor. Only prepped surgical teams were allowed to pass over it.

They stopped to put on blue surgical caps and masks. Dr. Luciano explained how to tie the mask on and pinch it around the nose to make it stay in place.

"Symmetrical and snug," he advised.

Then he showed Terrance how to fold a cuff around the hem of the cap, to look cool.

"You gotta put on the cuff or it looks too plain," the doctor joked.

They stood at the start of a long hall, the intersection in Terrance's life. All that stopped Terrance was the red line painted on the floor. Dr. Luciano stepped over it, then remembered he needed his surgical magnifying glasses and ran off to get them. Terrance stood statue-still, his toes flush against the red line, careful not to tiptoe over.

"I can't wait," he said, breathless.

He stared at the line, at the starting point and the operating rooms beyond.

Rows of white lab coats hung on the walls to his right and left. Each bore the name of a surgeon. He glanced at them then dug his hands deep into the one he was wearing.

"It looks so much different than you see on TV," he whispered.

Dr. Luciano hustled back. "Let's go," he announced.

Terrance stepped over the line.

They headed to the metal sink where surgeons scrubbed in. Dr. Luciano told him how cool the brain and spinal cord look, then casually shoved open the door to the operating room, and Terrance followed.

The teen's eyes grew wide as he met the team. They welcomed him and warned him not to touch the sterile field. The patient had been prepped, draped, and opened.

Dr. Luciano invited Terrance to watch from a footstool at the patient's head.

Terrance climbed up, leaned in, and peered into his first brain.

Adjust your own oxygen mask before helping others, or you'll be of no use to anyone—including you.

Whenever the flight attendant gives the standard safety lecture, no one pays attention, but I stop whatever I'm doing and make myself watch. It's a welcome reminder to take better care of myself. I savor the part where the attendant holds up the oxygen mask and tells everyone, "If you have small children traveling with you, be sure to secure your oxygen mask before assisting others."

How often do you get permission to put yourself first?

Traveling parents aren't the only ones who need to heed that advice. Too many of us, especially women, are guilty of neglecting ourselves. We're raised to put our spouse, children, neighbors, and strangers, even jobs, first.

I once interviewed a psychologist from the Cleveland Clinic for a radio show about stress. Dr. Michael McKee said something I've never forgotten: "Don't have a double standard for you." You need to treat yourself as well as you treat everyone else. That lesson hit hard one day when I planned to go to yoga class and finally penciled it in on my busy calendar. I hadn't been to one in months and made sure I kept the evening free for me. Two hours before class, a dear friend called and needed a sitter. Could I watch her son that evening?

Sure, I said, and canceled my yoga plans. Why did she need me to babysit?

She wanted to go to yoga.

Arggghhh!

I got screwed out of going to yoga and I did it to myself, all by myself. I had a wonderful time visiting with her child, but I didn't stop and consult me before giving my time away.

I do it all the time. So do most women I know.

Years ago, the American College of Cardiology in Atlanta came out with a powerful report that said women are at a higher risk of death from heart attacks than men because they delay getting to the hospital for treatment. Women typically take an hour longer than men to get to a hospital once they experience symptoms of a heart attack.

That may surprise doctors and researchers, but it's no surprise to women. When a guy gets chest pains, he calls 911 and heads for the hospital. What does a woman do?

She decides the pain might indicate something serious, so she bakes lasagna, meat loaf, and a tuna casserole to feed the entire family for the week she will be in the cardiac care unit.

When she opens the fridge to put the meals away, she can't stand looking at the green cheese and fuzzy leftovers, so she tosses them all out and cleans the shelves. She packs everyone's lunches before packing for the hospital. As she stops in the bathroom to collect her toothbrush, she pauses to scour the sink, tub, and toilet.

She figures her family will run out of underwear in a day, so she throws in a load of whites and folds the clothes from the dryer. She leaves for the hospital once everyone has eaten, done their homework, and finished their chores.

On the way to the hospital, she drops her daughter off at soccer practice, returns the overdue library books, and signs up to help with the preschool reading program.

By the time she gets to the emergency room, she has a near-death experience. But instead of her own life flashing before her eyes, her children's and husband's lives zoom by.

Women have always ignored their pain and minimized their needs. We constantly keep a double standard for ourselves. We put ourselves last. We'd never treat anyone else as lousy as we treat ourselves.

How do we change? How do we put the oxygen mask on first?

First, give yourself permission to do so. Consider this your official permission slip to take better care of you. The care and feeding of you is up to you and no one else.

Dr. McKee offered a few solutions to try. Here are some of the takeaways from our conversation:

Take care of yourself: Don't have a double standard. Don't respect your commitments to yourself less than you do your commitments to others. Don't give yourself away so there's nothing left of you for you. Don't pencil in time for you, put it in ink.

Take five: Stop and take five minutes to get calm, centered, and clear. Before picking up the kids after work or stopping at the store, sit in the car and be still. Reboot. You'll make better decisions and discover you really aren't the axis on which the world spins. What a relief.

Take six breaths a minute: I suck at breathing. Dr. McKee suggested taking just six breaths every minute. Inhale for five seconds, then spend five seconds exhaling. Try it. It's amazing.

Take it back: Don't hand the remote control of your emotions to others. No more blaming: "That guy is driving me nuts...My boss is giving me an ulcer... The kids are giving me a migraine." Take back the remote and keep pressing CALM. You can't control what others do, but you can control your emotional reaction to them.

Take a breather all through the day: Pick cues for practicing your new breathing, like when you're stopped at a light, get an e-mail from your boss, or have to wait in line at the store. Take one or two ten-second abdominal breaths and say to yourself, "All is well, all is well."

Take a pleasure cruise: Every week set aside one hour for you. Make it your own personal pleasure cruise. Take an hour of beauty and go to the art museum, a jewelry gallery, or visit a flower shop. Take an hour of calm and listen to your favorite music, read a favorite poet, use your favorite bubble bath.

Take an hour of nature and soak up the sun, the sound of the rain, the glimmer of stars. If you can't do 60 minutes straight, give yourself three 20-minute gifts of pleasure.

Take a blessing inventory: When you're stuck in rush-hour traffic, look around and make a quick gratitude check. The car next to you is held together by duct tape. Ah. Be grateful for your car. The car in front has three screaming children. Om. Be grateful for the silence inside your car.

Take the short view: See life as a series of sprints, not one long endless marathon with no end in sight. In between the series of jaunts, rest and renew.

Aristotle separated the world into thinking, feeling, and doing. Dr. McKee said to manage stress well, one has to change in each of those domains. My favorite Aristotle quote is this: "We are what we repeatedly do." Try to make it a habit to love yourself as much as you do everyone else.

Put the oxygen mask on yourself first, and everyone around you will breathe a little easier, too.

*Instead of treating people the way
you want to be treated, treat people
the way they want to be treated.*

Most of us grew up learning the golden rule: Do unto others as you would have them do unto you. Treat people the way you would like to be treated.

As good as that sounds, that might not be the hallmark of good treatment. Too often we do things for people that we would like, but they might not value our help in the same way.

I once read about two sisters who tried helping their mom get through her cancer treatments by coming over and cleaning her house. They spent hours scrubbing every inch of the bathroom so the room would feel sterile and clean when she changed her dressings after surgery. But when their mom got home from the hospital and saw the sparkling clean bathroom, she felt hurt that they had invaded her privacy.

When I was in eighth grade, our class took up a collection to buy our teacher something special. We had no idea what to get her, so we raised enough to purchase a coat. We later found out she felt hurt when we gave it to her. She wondered why we thought her own coat was so shabby she needed a new one.

My mom once told us all that she wanted a small portable TV set for the kitchen. Just a tiny one she could set on the counter while fixing dinner and move from room to room if needed. My dad bought her a huge TV set that she couldn't lift. She was disappointed that he hadn't listened to what she needed. He was confused that she didn't like a TV that was bigger and better than what she wanted.

Lesson learned: Treat people the way they want to be treated. What's important to us might not be what's most important to that person we're trying to help. I've learned to simply ask, How may I be of help to you?

Susan Miller taught me to take it one step further.

When I met Susan, she was the concierge at the Renaissance Cleveland Hotel near Cleveland's Public Square. Her business cards called her Concierge Supervisor, but the title Cleveland's Welcome Mat was a better fit. Got a problem? Susan had the solution. You could always find her in the lobby of the hotel, phone tucked under her left ear, fountain hissing in the background.

Need your flight changed? Lost your luggage? Want tickets to a sold-out show? No problem. Like a genie, she granted your wishes. Everybody was a VIP to her. Her mission was to treat people the way they wanted to be treated.

There was never a typical day for Susan, who woke at 3:50 a.m. to get to work by 5, a half hour before she needed to. In 14 years, she was never late.

"Seriously, I don't do anything special," she told me. "It's just kindness. It's the way I was taught. My mother was the most wonderful soul. She raised us to have empathy and love. I hope I am her greatest legacy."

When one famous poet wanted a glass of white wine at 9 a.m., Susan found someone to pour it. When former Cleveland Browns quarterback Bernie Kosar needed a babysitter for his nephews, Susan volunteered. When one of the members of the Allman Brothers Band cracked a tooth, Susan found a dentist. When her coworker Ryan Craig had his parents stay at the hotel for their anniversary, Susan sprinkled rose petals on their bed.

Almost everyone had a Susan story to tell:

The Rocking Chair: A woman with a newborn desperately needed a rocking chair to soothe her crying infant. After finding out that the hotel didn't have one anywhere in the building, Susan brought a bentwood rocker from her own home for the woman to use.

The Bike: When the person who promised to lend his bike to a triathlete didn't come through, Susan lent the racer her bike. He finished in second place.

The Swimsuit: One day a woman walked into the hotel wearing a bathing suit, hysterical that someone had taken her clothes. Susan calmed her down by handing over her own spare jeans and T-shirt that she kept on hand.

The Specimen: One woman came to town to receive treatments for kidney cancer. She needed to get a urine sample to the hospital but had no energy to deliver it. Susan volunteered to drop it off.

The Orphans: A group of orphans from Romania were visiting one fall. They had never heard of Halloween, so Susan assembled 20 trick-or-treat bags for the children to experience an old-fashioned American Halloween.

The Patient: A boy named Johnny flew in from St. Louis to receive treatments at the Cleveland Clinic for brain cancer. When his father had to fly back home early, Susan spent her evenings at the boy's bedside so he wouldn't be alone.

The Bath: Actress Diahann Carroll's manager called the hotel to make sure the performer could take a milk bath. Susan searched for a local dairy to deliver huge vats of milk. She had it warmed before it was sent to the actress's room and poured into the tub. Ms. Carroll was more than surprised. It turns out her request was misunderstood. All she wanted was a handful of milk beads to throw into the bathwater.

The Purse: Everyone's favorite story starts with a couple from Chicago who came to the front desk frantic over a lost purse. They thought it might be at a McDonald's restaurant somewhere between Chicago and Cleveland. Susan took it as a dare. She got out maps, traced the couple's route, then called McDonald's corporate headquarters and got the phone numbers of every McDonald's along the interstate—all 30 of them. On the tenth call, she found the Fendi purse.

"I don't know who was happier," Susan told me. "I knew then I could do anything."

Maybe we all can, if we just find out what it is people want.

If you want to see a miracle,
be the miracle.

Being God can be a drag.

Not that I would know from personal experience, but after seeing the comedy *Bruce Almighty*, it's clear that the job is harder than most of us might imagine, what with all those endless prayers and pleas for help.

In the movie, actor Jim Carrey plays a frustrated TV reporter who gets stuck in traffic, gets fired, gets beat up, and gets stuck with a dog that constantly pees on his favorite chair.

"God, why do You hate me?" the reporter cries out.

I've never quite asked that question, but at some moments—days even—I've felt like I was the punch line to one of God's jokes.

Those days where you walk out of the house and realize too late that the elastic in your underwear has disintegrated.

Or you get lost on the way to a job interview, or a bird decides to relieve itself on your new silk blouse.

In the movie, God appears as actor Morgan Freeman and offers a challenge to the man who feels like he's the ant and God is the bully on the sidewalk sitting under the blazing sun holding a magnifying glass over the bugs as they squirm under the heat. He says, "You think you can do it better? Here's your chance." Then he lets the unhappy earthling run the universe for a while.

It's great fun at first, parting a sea of traffic and a bowl of tomato soup, erasing clouds and enlarging the moon, expanding a woman's bustline and letting everyone win the lottery, even though they only get $17 apiece.

Drunk with power, the reporter yells, "MY will be done!"

It's scary, but only because he voiced it. Most of us wouldn't be bold enough to say that aloud, but our will always seems like it would be so much more fun than God's. I used to struggle with turning my life and will over to God. I feared God would send me a boring life with little fun and no sex. Who wouldn't want to play God? Wow. Where would you start?

You'd have to do the obligatory ridding the world of poverty, disease, hate, and evil. Make the blind see, the deaf hear, the lame walk. You know, the Miss America stuff that the final victor promises at the pageant's end when she's holding a bouquet of roses bigger than a first grader.

How about this? Every child gets to be born healthy and childbirth is pain-free. (We'll deal with that little overpopulation problem it would cause another day.) Everyone gets to go to college for free.

Instead of two-day weekends, make them three days long. And everybody in the world gets a four-week vacation.

Women and menstrual periods? Major design flaw.

How about a world where men don't go bald? Where they really can read a woman's mind and buy her the Godiva chocolate for Valentine's Day instead of edible underwear.

A world where the Cleveland Indians win the World Series at least every ten years. No, make that every five. Okay, once in my lifetime would be nice.

The Bible could use a good editing to make it easier to understand and harder to misinterpret. Give Job a break before he loses his whole family and everything he owns. Leave out some of the pestilence and plagues.

Give those who live in Cleveland the kind of weather San Diego enjoys. Come on, we deserve a break. They got the ocean. Sounds fair to me.

Make it snow everywhere on Christmas.

Keep hair from growing out of the noses and ears of men and on the legs of women.

Extend October and those gorgeous long autumns by at least ten days.

Expand all hearts and shrink all egos.

The world could get along fine without fire ants, fleas, mosquitoes, scorpions, snakes, spiders, and roaches. Yeah, yeah, they're all part of the food chain. Speaking of food, let's banish brussels sprouts, cottage cheese, and eggplant from the face of the earth.

Same goes for tornadoes, hurricanes, avalanches, blizzards, earthquakes, and tsunamis. Surely even God cringes about letting E. coli, flesh-eating bacteria, and genital herpes slip off the design board.

In God's defense, none of us could have dreamed up rainbows, fire, music, dreams, stars, thunderstorms, sex, deer, the Pacific, the Grand Canyon, and Niagara Falls.

But is it too much to ask that on every birthday, we each get one wish come true?

I know, I know, "Thy will, not mine, be done." As God said in the movie, "You want to see a miracle? Be the miracle."

Good advice for all of us mortals.

Instead of looking for proof of God's handiwork in magic tricks, find it in the moment. Instead of looking for miracles from above, find them within. Instead of looking for heaven somewhere else, create a slice of it here. Instead of looking for a sign of God's presence in a burning bush, a lightning bolt, or a crying statue, be present, and you'll experience God everywhere.

Every time there's a tragedy or a problem bigger than any solution we can see, we tend to ask, "Where is God?" Imagine what would happen if we stepped up to the plate, each of us, and said, "Here is God. Right here in me; right here in you."

God is in each of us, in the midst of every tragedy and problem. It's up to us to call forth our greatest light and love and be the miracle, right here, right now.

11

Everyone matters to somebody.

John Wood has no birth certificate, unless you count the tired black Bible that holds proof of his heritage and the promise of his inheritance in its gold-trimmed pages.

He doesn't even know how old he is. A woman found him tossed in a Dumpster in New York City when he was a newborn some 70 years ago. She took him home, gave him a name, and raised him as best she could. The baby she rescued from the trash made his life a mission to help the homeless. For more than 20 years, he worked at the City Mission in Cleveland doing everything from making soup to making beds, all in the name of love for men who feel the most unlovable.

"I ended up with the homeless," John said, smiling at the irony of it. "My whole life has been one big miracle."

The men he helps don't know what to call him. He answers to Reverend Wood, Brother John, Woods, or Doc. If John had a résumé, it would show that he has been a social worker, truck driver, emergency medical technician, minister, and embalmer.

A pastor in Cleveland invited him to the mission, back when the homeless men were all old skid-row alcoholics. Now the mission, a modern complex of pristine buildings, mostly serves young men with drug problems.

When John started here as a minister, the mission had five employees. Now it has 62. John drove the broken-down bus, fixed leaky pipes, and burned the trash. He still has the knife one drunken man pulled on him long ago.

"Oh, what a time we had," he said, grinning. He recalled going down to the basement at the old location to burn rubbish and seeing hundreds of rats.

"They're gone now," he said, laughing. "I am, too."

I met him at his retirement party. He wanted to spend more time with his wife, Bea. He planned to keep the jail ministry going and to visit mentally ill offenders.

"I don't preach them into a corner," he explained. "They have concerns and hurts. I listen to them."

His ears look like small wings that stick out from a crew cut of white. A stripe of orange runs down the center, a reminder of the redheaded boy who found God at eight years old and never lost Him.

At a luncheon tribute, John sat silently with his hands folded on his lap while people praised him.

"John Wood was like a father to me and all the men in the program," one employee said to a chorus of amens uttered by folks who knew how often John took the men home or on outings to the zoo.

Another man told how John used the Bible like a story-book, sharing tales of hope. "He was like Moses," the man said. "The men in the program was like his people."

Then John came to the lectern and read words from the prophet Jeremiah that fit his life story and all those he helped to feel loved.

"'Before I formed thee... I knew thee,'" John read, "'I sanctified thee.'"

John told them he couldn't take credit for any of the men he helped save. "Though I preach the Gospel, I am nothing to glory of," he said.

Then he squeezed shut the old black Bible whose ribbon markers are mere threads and walked away, his head hanging low as if still bowed in prayer for some lost soul.

Everyone matters to somebody. That's the message everyone learns or teaches at the City Mission.

There's another man who practices that motto when he volunteers there. John Gulley doesn't preach it in words, but in haircuts. He can restore a man's dignity in 20 minutes or less. In his hands, a comb turns into a magic wand, scissors sprout wings, and homeless bums become gentlemen worthy of a splash of fine aftershave.

Step into his barbershop—the men's restroom—where John trims away hair that has slept on the streets, hasn't been washed for days, and sometimes houses tiny critters. The tall man with the long, warm, fatherly Bill Cosby face knows that the only difference between the man in the chair and everyone else is one bad decision.

John's hair is turning gray, but his thick eyebrows are as black as the robe he wears to cut hair. Two days a week, he slips on latex gloves and opens up shop next to the sink and the urinal. Sometimes he listens to gospel music while he cuts. When I watched him, the whir of clippers, the whistle of scissors, and the hum of conversation provided background music.

"He's very gentle," said Anthony, who came in with a thick Afro. Anthony tipped his head at the black, fluffy clouds at his feet, a year's worth of hair. John rolled the clippers over Anthony's head, dabbing gently to make a part. He shook some talc on a washcloth and wiped Anthony down.

"Good," Anthony said, looking at his fade, which was similar to a buzz cut but longer on the top. "Thanks."

The moment one man left, another stepped in. Some days John cuts 35 heads.

"How we doin' today, Bill?" John asked. "You want a bald fade?"

"Close but not bald," answered Bill. As black clumps fall, Bill closes his eyes and relaxes, and John talks about his customers.

"We all make mistakes," he said. "We just make different mistakes. They're no worse than I am. It's just the consequences. My dirt and wrong didn't hurt me like it did them."

"Do you want a part?" John asked.

"No, sir," Bill answered politely.

John has no training as a barber. He retired early from the United Parcel Service after 25 years and started volunteering at the Red Cross, donating blood and helping disaster victims. He cut hair for a few people from his church, then noticed how bad the homeless looked and called the City Mission to help.

"I pray every morning and ask God to guide my eyes, my hands, and give me strength in my legs because I know I'm not a barber. I ask Him to hold the weariness and tiredness till I'm done," he said, adding that no one complained about his work. "They say, 'I can live with it.'"

"Do you know the difference between a bad haircut and a good one?" John asked, then delivered the punch line. "Four days."

Don sat down and John fastened a black cape around his neck.

"He does excellent," Don said.

"He's being kind," John replied.

"I'm being truthful," Don insisted.

John has never taken a dime for a haircut. He never will.

"God as my witness, I would not do it for money," he said. "I don't like it. But I love doing it the way I do it. I just feel good when I'm done. Most of these guys can't afford a haircut. They're fresh out of jail. They can get aggravating, with all the panhandling.

"I used to be a really heavy drinker. I put it away, every day. I mean every day. One day God took it away. I used to love to swear, and then He took that away. He let me see how ugly it was."

With his ugliness gone, John is able to help these men find their inner beauty.

"The haircut is secondary," John said. "It's a vessel."

He trimmed the hair around Don's nose and handed him a mirror.

"I feel like a million," the poor man said to the handsome man in the mirror.

"Beautiful. That's beautiful."

*Speak up for others, especially when
they aren't present to speak
up for themselves.*

There are so many times in my life when I should have
spoken up but didn't.

While talking on the phone one day, a caller began telling me about the business he owned. He casually mentioned how cheap one customer was. "You would think his
name was Goldstein," he said, then drifted off into another
topic.

Inside of me, a voice screamed out: *Goldstein? Did he just
insinuate that Jews are tight with money—that old stereotype?
Aren't you going to say anything?* But not wanting to sound self-
righteous, I said nothing.

While on vacation, two brothers were teasing each other
on the beach. Their father got angry and took the one son
aside. He ordered the boy to stand. As soon as the boy did,
the man ordered him to sit. As soon as the boy sat, the father

ordered him to stand. The boy went up and down like an obedient dog until he began to weep.

For more than 15 minutes the boy was ordered up and
down. Everyone nearby watched the humiliation but did nothing. As the boy grew more upset, his brother began throwing
sand and toys at him and laughing. The father did nothing.

A voice inside me wanted to cry out to the father, "Stop!
Leave him alone." Another voice in me whispered, *That's his
son. It's their business.*

I did nothing.

While at a coffee shop in Cleveland, I ran into a group of
women. After some small talk, one woman told a joke that
could be perceived as racist. I was stunned. No one in the
group laughed, but neither did anyone speak up. Someone
quickly changed the subject.

A voice in me yelled, *How can you let her pass bigotry off as
humor? Say something!* Another voice scolded, *Don't make a
scene. You don't even know her. It's enough just to not laugh.* And
listening to the wrong voice, I said nothing.

Walking through a parking lot after a high school football
game in Kent, we passed some men in a souped-up car with
the word *Ford* displayed in huge letters across the back window. My friend loudly commented on what hicks they were.
A few minutes later, the occupants drove by and yelled a racial
slur at him. My friend was angry but never acknowledged his
own comment that provoked the incident. Not wanting to
make the situation worse, I said nothing.

One Saturday I was driving to a local Twins Day festival in
Twinsburg with another couple when a friend pulled up beside
us in his Porsche and joked about the babes he was going to

check out at the festival. He was interested in only one thing and graphically expressed how he was looking to find a twin set of large breasts, ha-ha. A woman in our car was furious at how he objectified women. I was the only other woman in the car. I wanted to join her objections, but I said nothing.

One night when I left a diner in Cleveland to see a play, I saw a family of five walking back to their car. Suddenly, the father kicked his son in the back. As the boy began to cry, I wanted to leap out and yell at the man to stop. But who was I to lecture the father? It could be dangerous. What if he was carrying a gun? What if he hurt the child worse after I left?

I can still hear my silence. Over and over and over.

Can you hear yours?

Far too many of us remain silent. Years ago I wrote an investigative story about a teenager in Rittman, Ohio, who had been arrested for killing his father. For years, Will Snyder had suffered constant abuse at the hands of his alcoholic dad, who also suffered from a serious untreated mental illness. Then one morning, on January 21, 1996, the quiet 17-year-old who had never been in trouble picked up a baseball bat and killed his sleeping father. As soon as the news broke, a stream of neighbors and friends called the police on the boy's behalf. They told the police about all the times they had seen bruises on the boy.

Neighbors had seen Will's dad hit him so hard the boy fell to the ground. Friends had seen Will with black eyes, bruises, and welts. After the police completed their investigation, 70 people had confirmed that Will had been battered for years by his dad. Will was convicted of manslaughter. The judge gave him five years probation. No one had spoken up until it was too late.

There's a famous speech that was given by Pastor Martin Niemöller about the failure of good Germans to speak up during the Nazi regime to defend the rights of others. It's a powerful message for us all:

> They came first for the Communists, and I didn't speak up because I wasn't a Communist.
> Then they came for the trade unionists, and I didn't speak up because I wasn't a trade unionist.
> Then they came for the Jews, and I didn't speak up because I wasn't a Jew.
> Then they came for me, and by that time no one was left to speak up.

Why don't we speak up?

Fear of being wrong. Fear of rocking the boat. Fear of being wounded.

Yet it is our silence that allows others to continue to be wounded.

The Reverend Allan Boesak of South Africa, who fought against apartheid, once said that when we go before God at the end of our lives to be judged, God will ask, "Where are your wounds?"

Too many of us will say, "We have no wounds."

Then God will ask, "Was nothing worth fighting for?"

Give birth to yourself every day.

The call came late one Sunday night, just after 9:30. The woman cleared her throat, then left a brief message on my voice mail at work after I wrote an upbeat column.

"I just read your article in Sunday's paper. I was born in the 1930s. My mother was unwed. I was put up for adoption and I was adopted. I would have preferred to have been aborted because I have never led a happy life. I am quite sure there are many, many people out there that feel the same way I do."

That was it. She hung up.

I played the message over a few times to discern whether she sounded angry or hurt or both. The woman wished that she had never been born. She had lived for more than half a century and her life had never been happy.

I wondered how she measured happiness.

Hadn't she ever seen a glorious sunset spread across the

horizon? How about hundreds of stars against a black sky? Had she never been kissed passionately?

Did she ever ride a bike down a hill with the wind blowing through her hair? Or wade in a creek and squish the mud between her toes? Had she never made an angel in the snow, read a great novel, won at gin rummy?

Did she measure happiness in moments or in years? It had to be years.

Perhaps she piled up all the years together and declared her life unhappy.

Maybe she never got over feeling abandoned by her biological mother. Maybe the people who adopted her were unkind or abusive. But none of us—even those of us who got two parents right from the start—are guaranteed absolute unconditional love and happiness. Life isn't like that.

It's more exciting than that.

We'd be miserable if we were happy all the time. It would be like having perpetual summer. We'd get bored with sunshine and blue skies every day of the year. That's why I love Ohio. We get the great mix of thunderstorms, blizzards, heat waves, autumn leaves, and snowball fights.

No one has an ideal life. But if everyone could throw their lives into a pile and trade, most people would grab their own back. I'd grab mine, with all its hurts and fears and desperate moments. I wouldn't want any less.

Did she really think she was better off dead? She wished she'd never been born. I thought about Jimmy Stewart on that bridge in *It's a Wonderful Life*, ready to end it all, and how that goofy angel named Clarence showed him how the world would have sorely missed him.

Maybe this woman had never done anything as dramatic as saving someone's life, but surely she had touched someone in all her years on the planet. And if she hadn't touched anyone, she could start now.

I wanted to tell her to start her life over. If your pain comes from unloving parents, get some counseling. Divorce your family and create a new one with friends who love you. Volunteer somewhere to ease someone else's pain.

I wanted to tell her to talk to God. And if God was a stranger or a mean being who judged her, get a new God.

I wanted to tell her that even people who had two parents who loved them fiercely and protected them always were not guaranteed happiness. No one's every dream is realized. And if it is, it's usually after life kicks them around awhile.

I wanted to tell her to kick life back. If she hated her job, get a new one, or at least a new attitude. If she was bored with her home, rearrange the furniture. Paint a wall. Knock one down.

I wanted to tell her to rewrite her life. Make it a do-over. Wipe the slate clean every day. Start with a fresh canvas in the morning and paint madly each day without worry, without fear.

But I couldn't tell her anything. The woman left no name, no phone number. Just a bit of her misery behind, and an important message: happiness is a choice. Sometimes it's one I don't take. I wallow in self-pity, fear, anger, or sadness. When I find myself there, I stop and ask myself, *Do you want to be happy?*

Sometimes I surprise myself, because the answer is no. But when I say that word *no*, it's crystal clear I am choosing to be unhappy. My pity party doesn't last long, because I know it's up to me when the party ends. Sometimes I end it by simply going to bed early.

In the morning, I have a chance to be reborn, to give birth to myself. Who doesn't love a newborn? There's no judging a newborn. They're perfect as is.

My friend Don Cozzens, a Catholic priest, once ended a sermon with these words: "We are not broken people who spend our lives mending; we are born whole and spend our lives discovering that."

Why not discover your wholeness every day in the mirror? Claim your birthright. Discover the truth in those wonderful verses from Isaiah: "I have called thee by thy name. Behold, I have graven thee upon the palms of My hands."

What do you see when you look in the mirror? I want to see what Jessica sees. She's the little girl made famous in a You-Tube video for jumping on the bathroom counter and shouting affirmations in the mirror.

In Jessica's "Daily Affirmation," the five-year-old with wild curly blonde hair stands on the bathroom countertop clad in pajamas, feet straddling the sink, as she gives a pep talk to the mirror.

"My whole house is great. I can do anything good. I like my school. I like my dad. I like my cousins. I like my aunts. I like my mom. I like my sisters."

She gets on a roll, pumping her tiny fists. "I like my hair. I like my haircuts. I like my pajamas. I like my stuff. I like my room. I like my whole house!" Then she claps her hands as if she's ready to tackle the world.

"My whole house is great. I can do anything good," she says as she climbs down from the counter, past a potty chair and a tub full of toys. "Yeah, yeah, yeah, yeah, yeah. I can do anything good, better than anyone!"

Who doesn't want to feel that great every morning? Some might think reciting affirmations is the silly stuff of Al Franken's character Stuart Smalley on *Saturday Night Live* telling himself, "I'm good enough, I'm smart enough, and, doggone it, people like me." But research shows happiness is an inside job. Dr. Sonja Lyubomirsky, the author of *The How of Happiness: A Scientific Approach to Getting the Life You Want,* studies human happiness. Her research shows that life circumstances account for 10 percent of our happiness.

That's it?

Yep.

Genetics makes up 50 percent.

The rest? It's all up to you.

What if you gave that 40 percent 100 percent?

Linda Wisler Luft, who runs Fireball Coaching and Consulting in Columbus, Ohio, used to feel stuck. A cancer scare knocked it out of her. She's made a career out of getting others unstuck. She advises people to look at how they currently view their lives. Examine your current perspective, then choose a new way to see your life. Decide what you don't want and what you do want.

She encourages SMART goals: Specific, Measurable, Achievable, Realistic, and Time-targeted. Try to visualize each goal as if you had already achieved it. Picture yourself 20 years down the road. What do you want your future self to look like? Then give birth to it, every day.

Every morning look in the mirror and affirm the miracle that you are right now, as is, then step into your day and watch what happens.

Sometimes it's enough to make one person happy.

If you saw the Jack Nicholson movie *About Schmidt*, you had to wonder halfway through the film if the man's life really did matter to anyone. The payoff came at the end of the movie, when, in the wreckage of his life, Schmidt realized that he mattered to one child.

Sometimes we're so busy trying to make everyone in our lives happy, we don't realize that maybe it's enough to make one person happy. My friend Kevin Conroy, a Catholic priest, lives by the motto "Start with the poor." He has worked as a missionary priest in El Salvador and in Cambodia. He's the guy who gets the checks people in America write to help children who need food, books, or medicine.

I met him in 1986, when I set out in my first job as a journalist to change the world. Instead, I got stuck covering zoning board meetings about how high a fence could be built in a backyard in Lorain, Ohio. Boring. Then the newspaper wanted to do a series on poverty. I jumped on it. Where do you go looking for the poor? Everyone I met said, "Talk to Kevin. He knows where all the poor are."

Father Kevin took me all over Lorain, Ohio, down to the railroad tracks, to motels, to soup kitchens. There were poor people everywhere. How could I have missed seeing them?

He went on to volunteer in El Salvador and then Cambodia. He taught me that we should never forget that small acts of love are what ministry is all about.

"I live in the dollar-a-day world," Kevin says. In Phnom Penh, he works with the Little Sprouts, children orphaned by AIDS. All 270 of them are HIV-positive. The youngest one is 3; the oldest is 18.

When Kevin left them to visit his family in Cleveland, the children wept. They feared they'd never see him again. In their world, when someone leaves, they never return. Once when he left for the airport, the children held a raffle to see who would win and get to ride with him in the car.

Kevin's philosophy is that sometimes it's okay to give fish before you teach people how to fish. If we don't give them fish, he said, the kids with AIDS won't live long enough to be taught how to fish. He believes that serving the poor means you go where you are needed but not wanted and stay until you are wanted but not needed.

One of my favorite Kevin stories was the time he went to Honduras to bring help after a hurricane struck. Three days after Hurricane Mitch hit back in 1998, organizations were scrambling to collect medical supplies, aspirin, antibiotics, bandages, and other first-aid equipment. People were randomly dropping off supplies at churches and airports. People felt a huge need to respond.

The storm had dropped five feet of water on Honduras in five days. It changed the land and the people forever. The storm took more than 19,000 lives.

The people of Honduras needed medicine, not toys. A giant toy doll didn't belong, but the woman at the airport had insisted the doll go. The woman had been packing up goods for victims of Hurricane Mitch when her children took the doll from her bedroom and put it with the supplies. No, she told them, put it back. The doll had been hers since childhood. The doll was staying.

Three times she turned around, and three times they sneaked the doll back with the supplies. The fourth time that she saw it, she hugged it and cried. The doll was going.

She took the supplies and the doll to Martha Ponce, president of the Honduran Association in Cleveland. The woman held the doll to her chest and told Martha how much it meant to her and insisted it end up in the arms of the right child.

Martha wasn't planning on going to Honduras, but joined others on a five-day mission of mercy. She had left her homeland there 23 years earlier. Kevin came, too. George Muehlheim, a paramedic with the Cleveland Fire Department, was inspired to go after seeing the devastation on TV. Like all of them, he felt fortunate and wanted to give something back to others.

When Kevin and George met at the airport, they weren't sure what to make of the doll, which was as big as a toddler and stuck out among the suitcases, boxes, and backpacks of antibiotics, hydration fluids, and other donated medical supplies from area churches and drugstores. Why bother to bring it?

The woman who donated the doll had promised, "You will know who to give it *to*."

I don't think I will, Kevin thought, rolling his eyes at such magical thinking. The doll with the long blonde hair wasn't even culturally appropriate for a Honduran girl.

Kevin got stuck with the doll first. It sat on his lap on the airplane. The plane was full of first responders, people in Red Cross uniforms, even rescue dogs. When they arrived in Honduras, they set out in different vehicles. So much had been destroyed, it took the whole day to get to their destination.

Kevin squeezed the doll in with him and three others in a taxi the size of a Volkswagen Bug. They lugged the doll across a riverbed full of rocks and boulders. They dragged the doll 30 feet up a hill on a makeshift ladder that bowed with each step. Kevin wondered more than once why they were lugging the doll around. He whispered under his breath a few times, "What are we doing with this damn thing?"

The answer came when they met the eight-year-old girl who had been telling everyone, "Somebody is bringing me a doll."

At nightfall, they arrived in the village of Jutiapa, which still had no electricity. The team planned to drop off supplies at area clinics and help distribute them to treat the sick. First they stopped at a church where Martha told the priest and two religious brothers about the doll. All at once, the three men said one word: "Kaila."

Kaila?

She was a poor girl who had not been doing well, even

before the hurricane. She had volunteered at a makeshift shelter in the village after the hurricane. When 200 people showed up to eat, Kaila had stayed and washed dishes. She stayed the next day when 300 showed up, and again days later when 400 came.

Kaila's family had lost everything in the hurricane and was staying with relatives. They didn't have much to begin with in their mud hut, which was destroyed. She was so poor, she had no toys, not even a doll to play with. The other girls excluded her in their games, teasing her and turning her away for being so poor.

Shortly after the teasing, Kaila had a dream: Somebody was bringing her a doll. She woke up excited and described the doll to her mother. She told the kids at Bible school. She told the priest at her church.

Her mother promised, "Someday I will have money to buy you a doll."

"No," Kaila protested. "Somebody is bringing me a doll."

When she saw the doll, the barefoot girl wept. It looked just like the one in her dream. It had the same long hair, ponytails, bows, and flowered dress.

"Mommy, Mommy, I told you," Kaila cried.

Everybody was in tears.

Kevin was amazed. "We thought our mission was all this medical stuff. Maybe our mission was to make one child happy," he told me.

Sometimes the things you think are worthless and unimportant have the most profound impact. You can't make everyone happy or solve every problem. But you can make one person happy, and that is good enough.

The secret of life is no secret.
It's sprinkled all over your life.

W hat's the secret of life? What does it take to be happy?

Getting a raise?

Nope.

Retiring with a huge nest egg?

Strike two.

Winning the lottery and moving into a dream mansion?

You're out.

It seems as though every year the experts conclude that extra money will not make you extra happy. Of course, no one wants to be poor, but once your basic needs for food, shelter, and education are met, the extra money doesn't buy happiness.

Bottom line? Size matters—paychecks, that is—but not as much as you might think it does, according to happiness researchers. Yes, there really are economists and psychologists who get paid to study happiness. My guess is they're pretty happy.

Happiness is a hot topic. A report in *Science* magazine showed that people with higher incomes didn't report being happier; they reported being more likely to be anxious or angry. Another article I read said that having children, being retired, and owning a pet do not affect happiness. The article didn't say what happens if you experience all three.

The experts concluded that your outlook shapes your life more than life shapes your outlook. You can't control what happens to you, but you can control your response to what happens.

What's the secret to life? According to the movie *City Slickers*, it's one thing. What is the one thing? You have to find out. In the movie, three middle-aged men are searching for their smiles. They ultimately learn that the secret of life is one thing. They never tell you what it is. You have to find it for yourself.

How do you find that one thing?

The experts offer these tips for harnessing happiness: Choose time over money. Meditate and pray. Make peace with the past. Spend more time socializing with friends. Seize the day, the moment, the Oreos. Okay, that last one was my tip.

People used to turn to spiritual directors for the answer. Lately they've been turning to life coaches. My money is on the monks who say the secret is to find God in the present moment. If you do that, you'll discover the secret of life is no secret.

It's a baggy pair of overalls. Poems by Mary Oliver and Billy Collins. Music by Louis Armstrong. Chocolate by Godiva.

It's listening with both ears. Asking someone to dance. Driving with the top down. Loving the reflection in the mirror. Waiting up for your parents. Giving everyone a chance. Not counting strikes or foul balls. Not keeping score. The cool side of the pillow. Waterproof mascara.

The secret of life is knowing no one gets out of here alive. Loving every minute. Carrying a spare. Remembering to check your oil. Wearing cotton. Knowing when to let go. Holding a newborn. Laughing when you're happy. Crying when you're sad. Getting out of the way. Leaving notes in a lunch box. Daring to be different.

Having no regrets. Loving God regardless. Making peace with dandelions. Having friends who are computer literate. Charging less than expected. Loving a child. Complimenting your boss. Smiling at customers. Teaching someone to spell. Making cookies from scratch.

Showing up with flowers. Reading the funny pages. Skipping class. Starting with dessert. Wearing red underwear. Burning the good candles. Never growing up. Never growing old. Country line dancing. A squeaky porch swing. Saturday morning cartoons.

The secret of life is forgetting what you were mad about. Toasting the newlyweds. Speaking up for yourself. Praying for others. Playing peekaboo with a baby. Flipping the mattress. Hiring a maid. Wearing comfortable shoes. Knowing the mail carrier's name. Letting traffic into your lane. Singing Christmas carols in July. Taking walks that go nowhere. Watching Gene Kelly and Fred Astaire dance.

Thick chocolate milk shakes. Twelve-step meetings. Decaf after 8 p.m. Trips to the ocean. Merry-go-rounds. A swimsuit you can bend over in. SPF 30 sunscreen. A warm pair of gloves. Group therapy. Bubble baths by candlelight. Flannel pajamas. A pack of 64 crayons. A song in your heart.

Obeying the speed limit. Returning what you borrow. Pruning your apple trees. Leaving big tips. Paying bills on time. Not getting bees mad. Honoring your wedding vows. Performing somersaults in the front yard. Thanking a teacher. Getting on your knees to pray. Being persistent. Ordering takeout. Letting your employees leave early.

The secret of life is rolling down hills. Having grass fights. Singing in the rain. Receiving real letters written in cursive. Knowing where all the bird's nests are. Leaving spiderwebs alone. Asking stupid questions. Wishing on falling stars. Never going to bed angry. Asking for help.

Butterfly kisses. Winnie the Pooh. Campfire songs. Open sunroofs. Rides in the country. New socks. Tire swings. Recess. A bowl of cereal before bed. Fireworks. A good novel on the nightstand. Drive-in movies. The Serenity Prayer. Someone to confide in. A fat, juicy peach. Teddy bears with one eye.

The secret of life is saying "I love you" first. Telling the truth. Giving candy to trick-or-treaters. Reading the classics. Framing your photographs. Forgiving all debts. Carrying a camera. Making scarecrows. Using words everyone can understand. Checking the batteries. Not having to be right. Admitting when you are wrong.

Long walks in the woods. Riding a horse in the rain. Snow days. Karaoke. A new pair of shoes. Old pictures. A big, crunchy apple. Hayrides. Childhood games.

Being happy for the person who wins even when it isn't you. Honking the horn. Sticking up for your best friend.

Calling just to say hi. Writing a letter that starts out slow and ends up being five pages long. Crossing the state line. Sitting up all night talking to your mom. Trying not to laugh when you're already in trouble.

Jeans that fit just right. Fudge. The love of a grandparent. Adrenaline. The first snowfall of the year. Family reunions. Psalm 23. Eskimo kisses from a three-year-old. A grilled cheese and tomato soup on a cold day. Puppies. Snow angels. The fresh scent of new sneakers. The smile on someone's face when you do something unexpected.

Playing the license plate game. Watching old movies. Sitting on the front porch during a thunderstorm. Walking barefoot in the grass after a summer rain. Trying something new. Doing nothing for a day. Carving pumpkins. Treating people with respect. Knowing the consequences before you act. Calling in sick.

The secret of life is knowing that you alone make everything come true. Following your heart. Having faith in yourself. Being free to do what you want when you want. Remembering who you are and where you came from.

The secret of life is no secret. It's sprinkled all over your life. It's celebrating what already is. Right here. Right now. All around you.

If you can't be the rock,
be the ripple.

Majok Thiik Madut escaped Sudan's civil war, fled the bullets of rebel soldiers, crossed raging rivers of crocodiles, survived lions and hyenas, blazing sun and blistering sand as he walked across miles of desert to find safety in America, only to die at a bus stop in Cleveland, Ohio.

He and the other Lost Boys of Sudan fled their homeland in an almost biblical way, orphaned, homeless, possessing nothing but each other. Together they endured years in refugee camps in Kenya with no family and no place to call home.

The Lost Boys lost count of how many people they saw die. They lost track of their families as everyone fled in the chaos. They don't know why or how they survived when so many others didn't.

Nearly 30 of the Lost Boys came to Cleveland to live the American Dream. They came through a State Department relocation program in 2001. When they landed, they saw white covering everything. *What a strange kind of wheat*, one Lost Boy thought until he scooped it up and it melted in his hands. They had never seen snow.

A settlement worker found the Lost Boys cheap housing and menial jobs, then cut them loose. The Lost Boys had no one to help them understand their new world. They mistook a refrigerator for a closet. One thought the elevator was his room. They learned English by listening to people and repeating their words. They depended on the kindness of a handful of strangers. A few found volunteers to give them rides, to teach them to use a computer, to finish high school degrees. But for the most part, the boys were lost, until they lost one of their own forever.

Two weeks before Christmas in 2006, Majok Madut was shot and killed as he waited for a bus. He was 26 years old but seemed to still be a boy. He had asked for cookies for his birthday.

At the funeral, the Lost Boys wore baggy suits that puddled over borrowed dress shoes as they shuffled alongside the silver coffin. They helped the priest spread a white cloth on the top of the casket then smoothed it out slowly and gently, as if it were a bedsheet to help him rest. The tall, thin men held back tears behind their chiseled cheeks.

The Reverend Bob Begin asked forgiveness for what the community had failed to do. "We didn't build a more peaceful city for you to live in," he told the Lost Boys. "We beg you not to leave us. We beg you, stay."

Majok's brothers sang him to sleep, sang low and deep, their voices rising and falling as a single wave, like the chanting of holy monks. Then the congregation sang the song "Be Not Afraid." The words meant so much more this day: "You shall cross the barren desert, but you shall not die of thirst. You shall wander far in safety, though you do not know the way . . ."

At Calvary Cemetery, they lowered him into American soil, planting him in a place still not quite home. In Dinka they sang, "The place you came from you go back to." They prayed God would take Majok there.

After the funeral, they gathered for lunch in the church hall, their faces wet with tears. The other mourners wondered what to do next. How could they help the rest of the Lost Boys?

The Lost Boys told me they wanted challenging jobs that would cover rent and college tuition. "We work hard," Akol Madut said. "I don't have my mother. I don't have my father. The job—that is my father. That is my mother."

Amiol Arop was scared. "If somebody lead us, we can do it," Amiol said. "We got all qualifications. We are struggling. We are worried how we are going to survive."

Aleu Athuai told me, "We are confused. We don't know what to do."

Soon after Majok's death, a Catholic nun who had tried to help the boys had a strange feeling that something good was going to happen because of Majok. Sister Mary Frances Harrington, a sister of St. Joseph, told them Majok was going to give them a wonderful gift. Somehow she could see the holy in the horrific.

The nun held on to that spark. In time, hundreds of volunteers fanned it into a flame. Everything changed for the Lost Boys when a high school history teacher teamed up with the nun and decided to be their rock.

Tim Evans, a history teacher at St. Ignatius High School, invited anyone interested in helping to attend a community meeting a month after Majok died. More than 150 people showed up. Men in suits. Teenagers in sweatshirts. Mothers holding babies. Little girls with palm-tree pigtails. Elderly nuns with holy smiles. The stream of humanity flowed into the library where Tim coordinates social justice programs, where they practice the motto of the Jesuits, "For the Greater Glory of God," where students are taught to "be a man for others."

Tim did not have the Lost Boys attend the meeting. He was afraid they would lose hope again if people showed up and then did nothing. "This is our moment. This is their moment," Tim told the crowd. "Let's work for the greater good of these guys."

A big Cleveland police officer shook a tiny nun's hand. He wanted to teach the Lost Boys street smarts and how to understand American laws. A woman who sold real estate wanted to transform an apartment building to house them. An attorney offered to help with legal issues.

Some people decided to be the rock; others, the ripple. Some did great things, some did small things. A community formed around the men. Hundreds attended potlucks, game nights, and meetings. An army of volunteers stepped up to write résumés and cover letters, drive them to job interviews. Mentors taught them to drive, to use computers, to speak English. They found jobs and apartments for the boys and raised $93,000 to help pay for college, citizenship, and basic needs.

The ripple effect took off. Dimple Dough Inc. launched a website for them at www.sudlbc.org. Whole Foods hired 12 of them. St. Ignatius High School offered mentors and volunteers.

The men became U.S. citizens. They pursued college degrees and careers. They found wives and started families.

A church raised money to bring one of the Lost Boys' mothers to America. When the government denied her travel documents, the church helped her travel from Sudan to Kenya to telephone her son, David. It had been 20 years since he had heard her voice.

Amiol Arop enrolled at the local community college to become a math teacher. "I am staying here," he said. "I feel at home here. It is a good city."

Malong Mabior passed his GED and enrolled in community college to study accounting. He started a project called Isaac's Wells so the people of Sudan wouldn't have to walk miles to get drinking water.

Peter Dek became a pilot so he could work for the United Nations Refugee Relief Services and rescue other refugees.

Akol Madut published a book of his life called *Sleeping with the Sun in His Eyes: A Lost Boy at Home in the World.*

In time, the men became a rock for others, sending out ripples of hope.

The rock on Majok's grave summed up the story of his short life. The tombstone engraving was going to end with the words *Lost Boy of Sudan*, but the boys knew that Majok was not lost anymore, and neither were they. They insisted that one more line be added. His headstone now reads:

BELOVED SON AND BROTHER
MAJOK THIIK MADUT
LOST BOY OF SUDAN
FOUND BY GOD

Give as if the world is your family, because it is.

Everybody has a story about giving gone awry.

One winter, a boy rang our doorbell around dinnertime, offering to shovel the walk for $5. I had never seen the boy before and asked if he was from the neighborhood. He wasn't, but wanted to earn some money. I told him to go ahead. Then I noticed he wasn't wearing gloves and it was 20 degrees out.

As the boy began to shovel, I hollered upstairs to my husband, "The kid who wants to shovel doesn't have any gloves. Can I give him a pair you don't use?"

"Sure, just not my good leather ones," my husband yelled back.

"How about these red-and-black ones?" I yelled, holding up a pair of thick ski gloves.

"Fine," he yelled down, not really hearing me.

I gave the boy the gloves. Later my husband asked which gloves I gave away. When I described them, he cringed.

"You mean my good leather ones?"

Oops.

I felt bad until an hour later, when we went for a drive and we saw the boy, still shoveling walks, but with warm hands.

There are times when it's not so clear when to give. Almost everyone I know has been scammed by a guy who asks for $5 and claims his car has broken down. There's never a car in sight, and once the man has the money, he continues to ask others for the same $5.

So how do you know when and how to help people? What's the best way to give?

I once wrote a column about a woman facing eviction. Readers sent thousands of dollars, more than enough to pay her back rent. But I had to tell the next ten people who called seeking my help that I couldn't tell their sad stories. There were simply too many.

We're all bombarded with pleas for help: Do you give locally or globally? To the poor in South Africa or around the block? To needy family members or complete strangers?

After I gave away my husband's gloves, he gave me a lecture about Maimonides. The great medieval Jewish philosopher listed eight levels of giving, leading to the highest form of charity.

Give, but give grudgingly. Give with a smile, but give less than you should. Give an adequate amount, but only after being asked. Give before anyone asks. Give when you don't know the recipient. Give anonymously so the recipient doesn't know who gave. Give when giver and receiver are anonymous to each other. Give time, education, or money so that the receiver becomes self-sufficient. Follow the old saying, "Teach a man to fish, and he eats for a lifetime."

So maybe giving the gloves away wasn't such a bad idea. If only they'd been mine to give.

My friend Susan taught her nephew the gift of giving by handing him $100 at Christmas. Half was for him; the other half was for him to give away. Some churches give away $100 bills to people in the pews and ask them to find creative ways to give.

Father Charlie Diedrick at St. Barnabas Catholic Church in Northfield, Ohio, gave away $10,000 one Sunday. It wasn't the church's money, it came from one of his parishioners who had read *The Kingdom Assignment*, a book by a California couple who handed out $100 bills to 100 people. The couple said it was God's money and asked everyone to invest it in the Kingdom.

Father Charlie wasn't sure what would happen if he tried to send his congregation on a mission from God. Would anyone accept? He stuffed a wad of $100 bills in his pocket one Sunday and found out.

"Normally when people see the pastor approaching the pulpit, they figure they're going to get another money talk," he told them. "Well, this has a little different twist today."

He waved the money in the air and asked them to go and do something creative for God. Children tugged on their dads' coats and urged them to accept the challenge. Weary moms felt driven to their feet. So many people volunteered, Father Charlie ran out of money. When one family expressed dismay at missing out, the man behind them pulled out $100 and gave it to them. Someone from Georgia who had come up for a baptism wrote a check for $100.

Father Charlie ended up giving out $12,000 that day. He multiplied it before it even left the church. The more he tried to give away, the more he got to give away. The parishioners met weeks later to report where it all went.

One family bought duffel bags, coats, blankets, hats, and gloves. They made bologna sandwiches and drove to downtown Cleveland to give five homeless people a gift.

One family raffled off an Italian feast for eight they would serve in their home, raising more than $2,000 for a local boy recovering from an accident.

One woman raised $1,700 for an orphanage. Another turned her $100 into enough money to cover six operations for children with cleft palates.

A Girl Scout troop raised $4,000 for a boy taking care of his sick father and a grandma raising five grandchildren.

One girl donated her money to buy Thanksgiving dinner for 55 homeless men. Another girl raised $1,400 for Make-A-Wish Foundation.

One woman sent hers to a man in prison who divided it among five men who had no families to bring them personal supplies.

One woman bought candles labeled Hope, Peace, and Love and gave them anonymously with prayer cards. One woman who was diagnosed with breast cancer four days after she took the money said the assignment helped her focus on someone else's trials. She collected $350 in gift certificates for a single mom with a nine-year-old boy. One family filled their van with diapers, food, and clothes and took them to a shelter for children.

Even though they spent the money differently, they agreed on one thing: they got more than they gave.

"You know that look in your children's eyes on Christmas morning?" one man said. "We saw it in the kids we gave things to."

As generous as they all were, when I think of giving, I think of a kid named Chance Riley. His mother named the last of her five children Chance because it was her last chance at having a girl.

Chance, who was a 17-year-old Wadsworth High School senior, was shearing sheep at a county fair in Medina, Ohio, when he heard an explosion. An antique steam engine just 200 yards away blew up, killing five people and injuring dozens. Chance joined the brigade of 4-H kids filling five-gallon buckets with water to pour on the injured.

Chance came to the fair to win Grand Champion Pig. Two days after the explosion, Chance showed the prize pig he had been raising all year, the one he'd invested $350 in, the one he'd fed morning and night and walked four times a day. After he won, the teen gave the prize money—all $4,180 of it—to the victims, even though he didn't know any of them.

He could have bought a car, a motorcycle, or a computer. He could have purchased every CD he ever wanted. He could have cleaned out the Gap and bought a new wardrobe. He could have covered some of his upcoming college expenses.

Chance never gave it a second thought, never thought of just giving a portion of it.

"It was the obvious thing to do," he told me. "We're all family."

He's right.

Everyone is either your student or
your teacher. Most people are both.

The young man stood on the corner, a man of 21, perhaps, talking to himself, to the passing cars, and waving something frantically in circles above his head.

The first time I saw him on my daily walk through the neighborhood, I nearly turned down a side street to avoid him. Was he crazy? Then I got close enough to see that he was a boy trapped in a man's body. He held a flying toy truck, with two broken pieces of blue paper plate taped on as wings.

At first I felt a mix of pity and sadness for him and his parents, that he'd never drive a car, never go off to college, never get married. Then I found myself walking down his street just to get a glimpse of him for the pure joy he exuded, this boy who could make trucks fly. I never learned his name or his age and never saw his parents. His home was the one marked by a convoy of battered toy trucks parked on the doorstep, toys that were meant to one day be outgrown but never will.

One day he zipped past me on his bike and hollered over the distant thunder, "You better go home. It's going to rain and rain." One time he was tossing a football in the yard to himself and warned me that if you play without a helmet and get hit hard you could end up with brain damage. I wondered how his brain had ended up damaged.

Or was it damaged? He laughed louder, smiled bigger, and played more intensely than anyone around.

I thought of all the people like him that I've encountered, people who I thought needed us. Perhaps we need them more.

Dorothy and Al Petzker have seven children. Two of them are mentally disabled. I wrote about Theresa when she competed in ice-skating at the Special Olympics. Those athletes taught me about unconditional love, about purity of heart.

"They're humble," Dorothy said. "They have no discrimination. Everyone is the same to them. There are some things she can't do. There are a lot of things she can do. There are some things she can do better than you and me. We are all retarded in some areas."

David Spurlock has Down syndrome. He transformed a Boy Scout troop. At his first meeting with Troop 321 in Hudson, Ohio, the rowdy 12-year-old with the short attention span ran around hitting and tackling the other boys. They couldn't understand his speech and were scared of him. But David ended up teaching Troop 321 as much as they taught him.

They taught him how to tie a square knot, a hitch knot, and a bowline knot. He taught them how to take time to listen, not just to hear. They taught him how to pitch a tent, administer CPR, and say the Pledge of Allegiance. He taught them humility, patience, and determination. They taught him how to find his way through the woods without a compass. He taught them how to find their way through life without limitations stopping them.

Every time David advanced to another level, the whole troop celebrated. When David turned 18, he became an Eagle Scout, the highest rank any Boy Scout can achieve. Only 2 percent of American Boy Scouts attain the rank of Eagle.

Dr. Steve Lawrence, David's Scout leader, said, "I don't know if David got as much out of Scouting as the boys got out of David being around. We're all richer from having David in that troop."

The students on campus who met six-year-old Sarah felt the same way. Sarah pretty much lived at Brady's Coffee Shop near Kent State University. Her disabilities helped every college student feel more at home in the world.

Sarah's mother, Bonny Graham, owned the popular coffee shop, but Sarah was its heart. Sarah grew up at Brady's. She hung in a pack on her mother's belly when she was two weeks old. She sat in the crook of one arm as her mother poured coffee with the other.

A pile of toys in the corner of the restaurant belonged to Sarah. So did the crayons scattered about. She used to ride her toy cart across the wooden floor, crashing into tables and chairs. She was a disciple of Barney the purple dinosaur. She'd grab the microphone onstage and sing, "I love you, you love me, we're a happy family," to college students. If they didn't applaud, she would. Students taught her how to set up a chess board. They painted her nails black. A skinhead named Lance slicked her hair so it stood straight up.

She didn't know what a stranger was. Sarah learned the sign language alphabet from a Sesame Street book so she could talk to a deaf child who waited at Brady's for the bus. She sat with grumpy old folks and asked them, "What's your name?" even if she knew.

She swept the floor, washed dishes, and climbed on milk crates in the kitchen to reach the coffee mugs for the regulars. No one was ever sure how old six-year-old Sarah was. She never grew bigger than a four-year-old. She was developmentally delayed, had heart problems, and attended a special school.

One day, as she was getting ready for school, her heart gave out. She died in her mother's arms.

The next day mourners filled the coffee shop. They talked about how they'd miss hearing the little girl sing, "Are you special, special? Everyone is special in their own way."

Her mom carried the anonymous note someone had written for Sarah before she died:

I don't know how old you are nor how to spell your name...or anything else about you except this: Just about every time I come in here you have already left your mark. If it is not the table with the crayons, coloring book, and cut-up papers, then it is the green tractor sitting in the aisle idling, waiting for you to jump on and drive it away. Every time I sit to study, your sweet little voice can be heard, usually laughing. I've heard your name thousands of times, being called by your mom, and seen you get into trouble with a customer wanting his/her piece of quiet. Not me. Every time you come up to me, I ask you your name and you ask me mine. I have read Dr. Seuss to you, and I'll never forget how you laughed from page one of *Cat in the Hat* to the page at the end. You have amazed me by how your little unbalanced legs have carried you up and down Brady's one flight of stairs so many times without falling. I hope you have a happy life. You have made so many people smile.

Bonny was going to tuck the note away and give it to Sarah when she turned 18. Instead, she made copies for all the mourners, Sarah's students.

Pray like you mean it.

A few days after I found a lump in my breast, I went to the doctor hoping she'd tell me it was nothing to worry about. She pressed her fingers there and said, "Yes, you have a lump." She set a mammogram appointment for the next day but didn't sound overly concerned. I wasn't worried until a nurse in the hall said good-bye and added, "I'll pray for you."

Pray for me?

Yikes. That's when it hit me that I might really have cancer. I sat in the car and cried. It couldn't be a lump. Not a real lump. Not the kind you read about. I imagined the worst: losing my hair, my breast, my life. Leaving my daughter, my stepsons, my husband. I looked in the rearview mirror and pulled my hair back from my face. No, I couldn't be on the verge of cancer. I would look hideous bald.

Sitting there with the car turned off, I went from zero to

death in five minutes. For the next two weeks, my heart beat too fast, my feet tapped nervously, my hands were so jittery I dropped things. I clung to the faith of my Catholic childhood, praying rosaries and psalms. The prayers were good for about 24 hours, then each one expired and all I heard within was the pounding of my own heart.

How did one pray at a time like this? I wanted to pray the right tumor-be-gone prayer. Should I think positive that it wasn't cancer? Or trust God completely regardless of the outcome? I was so afraid of praying the wrong way. I didn't doubt God had the power to heal me, but would God use it? I finally settled on the words "Thy will be done." Jesus surrendered in the garden of Gethsemane the night before His death with these words: "Father, if Thou be willing, remove this cup from Me: nevertheless not My will, but Thine, be done." I emphasized the "Remove this cup from Me" part to make sure God knew 100 percent that I didn't want cancer. When I prayed that way, I felt a deep peace, even after I found out it was cancer.

On the eve of that first chemotherapy, my plan was to accept this whole cancer experience as a spiritual challenge. I wished this cup would pass me by, but it had not.

The motto of the oncology department should be, "We put you through hell to get you well." My whole body took a beating. Mystery side effects showed up out of nowhere. Just when I managed to get one under control, another one emerged. Nosebleeds. A rash. Weird aches and pains. For weeks, I lived on mashed potatoes, scrambled eggs, and macaroni and cheese, the only foods bland enough to swallow. Toast hurt too much to chew. Chocolate tasted like metal. Fatigue rendered me useless. I tried exercising but had to quit when I kept seeing stars. My body felt too heavy to carry up the steps. After a shower I needed a nap to recover. My goals in life shrank to eating three meals a day and sleeping a whole night. My to-do list was down to survival basics: eat, sleep, shower, change couches.

Everyone else seemed so busy with life. I kept comparing my life to theirs and ended up feeling cheated. Everyone says there is power in prayer, but I was starting to wonder. After days of throwing a pity party for myself without anyone bothering to RSVP, I asked my husband, "If all these people who say they are praying for me actually are, why am I so sick?" My husband, a self-proclaimed agnostic, replied, "Maybe if they hadn't prayed you'd be a lot sicker." Well put.

One get-well card jump-started my faith. It read: "Gratitude is the mother of all prayer." It was time to stop focusing on every ache, pain, and side effect. It could be much worse. I thought of the woman who, after she read my newspaper columns about my cancer experience, sent me a photo of her bald six-year-old who was going through chemotherapy. One woman wrote to me about her husband's inoperable brain tumor and their two young children. Another reader had lost her only daughter in March and faced her first Mother's Day alone.

My daughter encouraged me to keep a gratitude journal. The more I wrote, the more convinced I was that people were praying me well. On nights when I couldn't sleep, I offered up a rosary for all of them. Each Hail Mary went to heal someone else. No more prayers for me, me, me. There was magic in that rosary. When I started praying for others, I started feeling better. I tried it the next night and the next. Instead of just keeping a gratitude journal, I began a new journal, a prayer journal. Not the kind where you write letters to God for what you want, but where you write in the names of everyone else who needs help. Instead of mentally replaying home movies of my woes, I listed their names and prayed for them. Every day I wrote in someone else's name, someone who needed a prayer more than me. I sent them a Hail Mary and simply asked, "May their burdens be lightened," then fell into a peaceful sleep, grateful not for what I had but for what I had been spared.

Years after that cancer journey, I discovered another way to pray that I now use every day.

One day I walked into a bookstore and wandered around the inspirational shelves and discovered four small books by an author named Ernest Holmes. I'd never heard of the guy. He changed the way I prayed for good. Too many of us, myself included, continually ask for help but never pause long enough to actually receive it. I had always prayed without ceasing but without real faith.

Let's say I call my friend Beth and ask her to have lunch with me on Thursday, and she says yes. Then I call her every 15 minutes to double-check if she wants to have lunch with me on Thursday. She'd start to wonder, *Why doesn't Regina believe me? Doesn't she trust me to show up?* That's how I've been with God. I'm an asker and a doubter.

If I'd had more faith, I would have trusted the prayer the first time I said it instead of repeating it.

Holmes suggested a new way to pray. First surround yourself with a God who loves you. I call it "surround-sound God." Then ask for what you need. Be specific about your concerns.

Leave no doubt. The Bible says, "Ask, and it shall be given you; seek, and ye shall find; knock, and it shall be opened unto you." It also says, "And all things, whatsoever ye shall ask in prayer, believing, ye shall receive."

I name exactly what it is I need. Since I don't always know what is best for me, I trust God does and add, "This or something better."

Then, and this is really where it all changed for me, I pause and acknowledge that I have complete confidence in a God who loves me. I consciously receive from God what I have requested. I take time to actually receive what I asked for. I had never done that before.

The last part of the prayer is to pause to give thanks. You act as if God heard you. Act as if you believe in the power of prayer. Act as if you can take God at His or Her word.

The only part of the prayer you ever repeat is the final part. Thank You. Anytime you start to doubt, you don't start the prayer all over again and beg God to address your needs. You simply believe God already heard and say, "Thank You for..." Some days I find myself combating fear by saying endless thanks.

From now on, I pray like I mean it. No more hitting SEND over and over. It's changed my life. It has freed me from fear and opened up endless avenues for me as a writer, radio host, parent, wife, and friend. It has enhanced every relationship I'm in, starting with the most important one: my relationship with God.

Real faith isn't praying without ceasing. It's believing that God heard you the first time.

Arrive early.

It's such a simple concept that most of us overlook it.

Think how it could change the world if everyone showed up early for work, school, airports, dates, weddings, child visitations, and family gatherings.

I used to show up late for everything: classes, concerts, church, movies, counseling appointments, work, lunch, dinner, and dessert with friends. It didn't matter if I wanted to be at the event or not, I was always late. If the event started at 9 a.m., I'd leave my house at 9 or later. I never calculated the time it took to get there. I never thought about the people on the other end waiting and wondering where I was or the people on the highway between me and my destination as I sped to get there.

Yet I hate waiting for people. Who doesn't? You start to get irritated and wonder if they'll ever show up. I have a 30-minute rule. If you don't show up within 30 minutes of our agreed-upon time, our plans are off. When I shared my time rule with Bruce, who later became my husband, he called from the road on his way to pick me up for our first date. I cringed when I answered the phone, figuring he was calling to tell me he wasn't going to be on time.

"You told me what happens if I'm thirty minutes late," he said. "What if I'm thirty minutes early?" That impressed me. A man who showed up early made me feel valued. Respected. Appreciated. It made me realize how I offered none of that to others.

A stranger at the airport convinced me that arriving early is a real service to others. He arrived at Cleveland Hopkins International Airport on a chilly day in Cleveland for a connecting flight home from wherever warm place he had been. He wore shorts, sandals, and a white T-shirt that showed off his vacation tan. He ran through the airport 20 feet ahead of his wife and son. He arrived at the gate just as the plane pulled away.

His glowing bronze tan turned a bright red. He was furious. He missed his flight. He started yelling at everyone around him. Anyone in a uniform became his target. His wife held her head down in fear. His son looked embarrassed. The dad was unstoppable. "You people are awful. I can't believe this," he bellowed.

He went on to blame the workers in security for slowing him down. The gate attendant who wouldn't let him on the tarmac. A flight attendant who walked by. Everyone was at fault except for him.

Because he was late, he did his best to ruin everyone else's day. I stood waiting for my plane with three strangers. We all shook our heads as we watched the man disrupt the life of every worker in the airport. "Arrive early," we said in unison.

Think about how arriving early could change the world: No more road rage. Everyone gives themselves enough time to arrive. Fewer speeding tickets. Everyone has enough time to factor in for detours and delays.

I used to be chronically late until a counselor pointed out that I needed to address my time issue. "You suck at time," she said. "You act as if it doesn't exist. It's like you live in a no-time zone."

She was right. I had an inner teenager on board who rebelled against being anywhere on time. I refuse to wear a watch and don't want to be boxed in by hours, minutes, and seconds. For the longest time I didn't respect time—mine or anyone else's. My mom used to always tell me, "You'll be late for your own funeral." That one I'm okay with. If you are going to be tardy, that's not a bad event to be late for.

The downside to being late? It upsets people when you're late. People see you as rude and disrespectful—and they're right. People think you're inconsiderate, incompetent, and self-centered—and they're right. You get a bad reputation. People think they can't count on you. If they can't trust you to show up on time, can they trust you to follow through with commitments? They don't take you seriously. Your word is no good.

Sure, you offer apologies and promises you don't intend to keep. You end up telling lies or half-truths about why you're late to make yourself look better. You embellish how bad the traffic was or how many blocks you got stuck behind the school bus or how slow the old lady was driving in front of you, when the truth is you were late because you overslept, tried to squeeze in one more activity on the way out the door, didn't leave in enough room between commitments, or never determined how long it would take to get to the event.

Being late causes stress for you and everyone else. It creates a roller-coaster ride of drama and adrenaline. I used to thrive on that cheap high until I realized that at the other end of my journey there was someone feeling low.

Being late hurts relationships. Imagine how awful your children feel when you're late for their school and sporting events. It's terrible to make them worry about whether you're going to show up and see them play soccer, basketball, or hockey. Or whether you'll arrive at their school play or recital to watch them perform their solo.

Then there are the divorced parents who are late to pick up their child for their weekend of visitation. The child stands at the window and watches in tears as each car passes and it isn't Mom or Dad. Why make them fret that you forgot them? Arrive before they're at the window. Put their minds at ease and arrive early so they know you value your time together. Don't let them think for a second that you don't care, that you won't show up.

Being late is a poor thing to model for them. Don't teach them to make people wait for them, that it's okay to make a grand entrance and get cheap ego strokes at the expense of others by walking in late.

I've seen people walk in late to funerals and weddings, which draws attention to them instead of the person everyone else gathered to celebrate or honor. So why are some of us chronically late?

"I'm a procrastinator," people will say. But what is that, really? I've heard it said that procrastination is just fear with a college education. It's a big word to describe why we delay doing something or refuse to do something. We avoid arriving on time out of fear of the people we have to meet on the other end, or we're afraid if we arrive too early, we might just have to spend time alone.

For some people it's a power game, a way to control others by making them wait. You get to hold up the spinning of their world. For others, it's a cheap way to rebel and create some drama.

Some people are chronically late because they can't say no and don't leave enough room for all the things they've said yes to. But are you really saying yes to something if you're going to miss it by being late?

The military has a motto: "If you aren't five minutes early, you're late." Then there's the old saying: "If you're five minutes early, you're on time. If you're on time, you're late. And if you're late, you're fired!"

Most people wouldn't consider being late for a job interview. You want to make a great first impression and walk in the door five minutes early. But once they get the job, they show up five minutes late every day and think nothing of it.

I've done a 180 on time. I'm not perfect, but most days I try to leave a 15-minute buffer between events. I schedule in breathing room. That gives me time to get a decent parking space, make calls in the parking lot, hit the restroom, relax, pray, pause, prepare, and just breathe. I figure out what time the appointment is, add 15 minutes, and factor in travel time, then work backward to figure out when to leave my house.

When I travel by air, I arrive two hours before a flight. In the old days, you could dash through the airport, run to the gate, and hop on the flight as the plane was pulling out. Not anymore. I leave extra room in case there's a high security alert, traffic on the drive, a flat tire, a tight parking lot situation, or long lines to board. It feels good to check in with room to spare to read a book, check e-mails, eat, de-stress, and prepare for what's on the other end.

I've also tried other tips friends suggested. Set the clock five minutes ahead. Check the weather the night before so you have your boots or umbrella at the door. Choose what you'll wear the night before, pack your lunch, fill the gas tank and wallet with cash for lunch or parking. I keep my keys in the same place every day, in a basket by the back door, so I never waste time looking for them. My husband taught me that trick. When we first got married, I wasted hours every week looking for my keys. He even bought me a clapper key ring that made noise when you clapped so you could find your keys. I lost the clapper.

The biggest change is to think through what I put on the calendar before the ink hits the paper. I pause before saying yes and ask each person what kind of time commitment this will involve. Then I pause and ask myself what I will be giving up to say yes to this. Everything is a trade-off. Every time you say yes, you are saying no to something or someone, probably you. I'm starting to say no more often than yes.

When it comes to completing tasks, I give each one an amount of time. How much time will it really require? That way, each day on the calendar isn't full of a stack of to-dos that can't possibly fit into a 24-hour day.

Instead of being predictably late, you can be the one most likely to show up early, the one everyone can count on.

Life is unpredictable, but you don't have to be.

Dream big.

W ish big.

That's what little Latanya was thinking the day the pink slips went out.

That's what a few hopeful residents in her poor inner-city neighborhood thought when they envisioned a new school for their children.

But first, Latanya's story.

That December, all the other children had quickly scribbled down what they wanted from the U.S. Postal Service angels who had adopted their school for the holidays. Latanya brought her pink request form home to give it more thought. When her mom offered to help write out her wish list, the six-year-old resisted.

"I'll do it," the first grader said, then asked her mom how to spell *shoes* and *clothes*.

Her mom never saw the form after it was filled out. The teacher collected the slips and turned them over to the post office, which bought Christmas presents every year for all the children in two needy schools in Cleveland.

Of the 1,272 pink slips from both Harvey Rice Elementary and Walton Elementary schools, Latanya's stood out. Most of the children wrote down that they wanted Barbies, G.I. Joe dolls, skates, video games, CDs, and coloring books. Latanya's list stopped the postal workers cold. The girl didn't ask for a doll, a stuffed animal, or a game. Under the words "This is what I would like for Christmas," she wrote: "shoes, school clothes, food, and a bed." The request left postal clerk Debbie Cockrell aghast.

There's no way a six-year-old should be asking for food and a bed for Christmas, she thought, then called the school to see if the child really needed a bed.

She found out the girl and her mom shared one bed. They had just moved to Cleveland from New York. The mom had no job. Debbie got busy. She bought $400 worth of toys, clothes, and food for the family and got everyone at work buzzing about finding the girl a bed. Word spread to distribution clerk Yvette Lucas, who had a wish to fulfill.

An only child, Yvette was heartbroken when her mother drew her last breath that September. Yvette stayed beside her until the end and thought the handful of dirt she threw on the grave was her final good-bye, but something felt unfinished. Her mom's last wish was to make sure all her belongings went to the needy. Yvette had donated 14 bags of clothes to a homeless shelter. She still had the Thomasville oak bedroom set her mom bought in 1982, the year her mother got cancer.

Her mom bought it in case Yvette ever needed to move back home. As soon as Yvette heard about Latanya, she knew it was time to let another piece of her mother go.

When Latanya's mother saw the truck pull up to their home, she gasped. "Oh, my God," she said, covering her mouth as tears began to fall. She held her hands in prayer as postal workers unloaded food, toys, and the bedroom set.

"I can't believe my baby did all this," she said. Yvette took one look at Latanya and told the girl's mom, "I pray you have the same relationship with your daughter that I had with my mother."

After setting up the dressers and making the bed, Yvette lingered to say good-bye. It was going to be her first Christmas in 44 years without her mother. She ran her fingers along the bare dresser top, the one a little girl would grow up to fill with perfume bottles and bows, lipstick and nail polish.

"Thank you, Mommy," Yvette whispered. "This is beautiful."

Latanya had a dream bedroom at last.

Unfortunately, she still had to wake up and go to a school that was physically a nightmare.

Harvey Rice Elementary School looked like an abandoned warehouse guarded by a ten-foot-high chain-link fence. The entrance seemed more like a dark cave. New teachers couldn't find the front door. Neither could I. Chicken wire covered the windows to catch the glass when it fell out. One time a window fell into a first-grade classroom, sending children crying into the hall.

In the winter, snow fell on the students. One day it was 38 degrees—inside. The kids wore their coats all day and the teachers stuffed newspapers in cracked windows to stay warm. The school had no playground, no PA system, no working water fountains. I spent the entire school year of 2002–2003 stopping by weekly to write about the school, walking up the three flights of crumbling black steps, under the water-stained ceilings, past holes in the walls, and around chunks of plaster that landed on the stairs.

I'll never forget standing on the asphalt parking lot playground watching students celebrate the last day of school, how they tied bright balloons to the rusty stairs by the ugly trash bins. A coalition of parents and residents decided those kids deserved better. After all, the school was named for Harvey Rice, the founder of public education in Ohio.

They wanted the school torn down and, after years of pushing and planning, got a new one built, one that would serve as an oasis from the poverty that brought drug dealers, gangs, and gunfire to their neighborhood.

The new Harvey Rice School was dedicated in 2009. The parents, library staff, school board, local development corporations, and foundations dreamed big and worked together to attract the needed money and support. The new school sits on a five-acre learning campus. It's connected to a new library that has a homework help center and computer lab. The school cost $16 million; the library cost $6 million. It took a collaboration of the school district, the library staff, various foundations, nonprofits, parents, and local artists. Together, the learning campus serves as the hub of the neighborhood. It's a model for what can happen when people work together.

Inside, bright walls offer portraits of success: Neurosurgeon Ben Carson. Photographer Gordon Parks. Poet Maya

Angelou. There is a music room, a science lab, and a computer lab. The principal wanted two computers. He got 29.

Classrooms have computerized "smart boards," not just chalkboards. There's a flat-screen TV, new carpet, elevators, air-conditioning, and an art room with three sinks and supply closets, not just a cart of supplies to push from room to room.

The children helped create murals on the walls. One child drew a graduation cap next to the word *dream*. The school motto hangs on one wall to inspire every Latanya who walks in the door: "What we believe we can achieve."

A bed. A building. Two wishes.

Both fulfilled when someone decided to dream big and make it a reality.

*Consult your own soul. Deep inside you
already know the answers you need.*

W e gathered one spring in Arizona for a sisters' weekend that changed my life. My sister Joan lives in Phoenix at the base of a mountain and invited us all out for some R & R.

For fun, we drove out to Sedona to wander around the gift shops and see the powerful rock formations in the city that is considered by many to be a spiritual vortex. One sister suggested we get our auras read. Why not? It was something fun to talk about. Whether there was anything to it or not, we'd find out later.

We crowded into a room in the back of a New Age gift shop and each took turns. We sat down, placed our palms down on a special panel, and the aura reader took our pictures. A form appeared in a blurry photo that looked like a big smear of colors. Each picture looked completely different.

The woman had something fascinating to say about each of us as she studied our auras. I don't know how she did it, but she was spot-on. One person needed to deal with anger issues, another needed to stop making work so important, another needed to start traveling. When she came to me, I told her I wasn't sure it would work, because I had a headache. I felt a migraine coming on and didn't know if that would interfere with my aura. I don't get them often, maybe once a year, but when I do, my vision blurs and, within 20 minutes, it feels like a sledgehammer coming down on my head. Then I'm sick to my stomach and my head throbs for a few hours before I pass out from the pain.

She studied me for a moment and asked, "Why do you have a headache?"

"I don't know," I told her.

"Yes, you do," she said.

What a jerk, I thought. Her tone stopped me cold. Maybe she was right. What if I really did know the answer? So I paused and asked myself, *Regina, why do you have a headache?* The answer I heard was, *Because you were in the sun and didn't wear a hat.*

Before I could answer, she said, "You need to wear a hat in the sun."

Bingo. That's when the headache had started. I had been sitting in the Arizona sun hours earlier at lunch and felt a funny tingling on my head but paid no attention. I ignored my body's little warning light, just like I ignore the engine light when it comes on in the car.

I don't remember a whole lot about what the actual aura said about me, but that woman taught me to listen to me, to go to myself first with questions, to consult my own soul, no one else. It's life-changing to believe that your body knows the answers you need.

It cut down on the migraines. Most of them came after I was in the sun too long. I keep a hat with me and almost never get the headaches now.

We really do know the truth deep inside. To really listen, you need to stop acting helpless and stop interviewing everyone else for answers. You have to take time and stay silent to listen to your own soul. Doing so has helped me heal my body and restore balance to my life.

What would happen if you really believed that your body knows the answers you need? What if it really does possess the answers to most of our questions?

Ask yourself what you need, and expect an answer. Doing this has never failed to help heal my body.

For years, I had trouble with my hands. It seemed like every journalist in the newsroom was walking around wearing wrist braces and suffering from carpal tunnel syndrome. I soon joined them.

My hands hurt from typing. Unfortunately, that's how I make a living. The pain gradually spread from my hands to my forearms, then traveled up into my shoulders. My girlfriend called it Yuppie Disease. I would have laughed at that if it hadn't hurt so much. It got so bad I had to sell my car. I could no longer shift gears, so I bought an automatic. I couldn't put a garden in because it hurt to shovel, hoe, and pull weeds. It's an embarrassing injury because it's invisible. One day a little boy asked me to lift his bicycle up onto a porch. He couldn't understand why I wasn't able to. My hands grew so weak I couldn't lift a gallon of milk.

The worst humiliation was in physical therapy. One day a tall thin man pedaled away on a bicycle next to me. He was a construction worker who was regaining the use of his legs after he had been crushed when a wall fell on him. He had been in a body cast for six months. "And what happened to you?" he asked.

I wanted to tell him that I injured myself doing something daring and dramatic like skydiving or rappelling. "I typed too much," I answered, embarrassed at the truth.

I ended up taking a nerve conduction test to find out what was wrong. It involved electric shock to the nerves in my hands and arms. The technician taped two electrodes on my arm, one with a red wire and one with a black. It reminded me of how you jump-start a car battery. A black stimulator with two metal prongs sticking out sent electric currents into the nerve pathways. Just before zapping me, she asked, "You've given birth before, right?"

The first shock felt like a powerful heartbeat. The next one felt like a hit to the funny bone. The third felt like the toy science generator we had as kids. The generator gave off miniature bolts of static electricity that we used to shock each other. The highest voltage the technician gave me wasn't quite as bad as the time I tried removing a broken lightbulb while it was still in the socket. I was chipping pieces of glass out of the socket with a butter knife when a jolt of electricity shot through my arm and knocked me to the floor.

The whole test was over in 30 minutes. It showed my hands suffered from repetitive stress injuries (RSIs). Basically, too much typing and too few breaks. I ended up reading every book I could about RSIs and decided to simply start listening to my body. When my hands get tired now, I stop typing. I set a timer for 20 minutes then take a break, leave the chair, and do stretches. I squeeze "power putty" to keep my hands strong. Gradually, they healed. Ever since I started listening to my body, my hands have been stronger than ever.

There was a brief period of time when my back caused me problems. I had a constant ache in my left side and random stabbing pains in my right side, like a knife jabbing me. It was shortly after I had finished radiation treatments for cancer, so I feared the worst. An MRI showed there was no cancer. Whew. It did reveal a disk with arthritis. Instead of giving in to that and seeing that as a weak spot on my body, I decided to stop, get quiet, and consult my own back. What did it need? Why did it hurt?

What I heard my back say was this: *You are trying to carry the weight of the world on me.* I was saying yes to everything and everyone. I was worrying about everyone's problems and trying to fulfill everyone's needs to the point of breaking myself.

I decided to say no more often, to reduce the load I put on myself. I do back exercises and stretches every day to strengthen the muscles around my spine and to stay flexible. I haven't had any pain for years. I honor and respect my back and pay attention to its warning light. If my back ever does hurt, I pause and ask, *What weight am I carrying that isn't mine?*

Every so often my life still gets out of balance. One summer, my jaw slipped out of place. For two months, my teeth didn't match. I had trouble eating and talking. I saw my dentist, who suggested it might be from stress. Was I clenching my teeth as I slept? I saw a jaw surgeon who did X-rays. What a relief to know there was no tumor causing the misalignment. He didn't want to do anything invasive to correct the problem and neither did I. He suggested a few ways for it to naturally fall back into alignment: Relax your jaw for a few weeks. Stop chewing gum. Don't chew on ice or hard candy. Apply heat around the area before bed. Gently massage your jaw and neck muscles.

I jotted all that down then came home and sat and meditated. I had forgotten to ask my own body what it needed. Why was my jaw out of alignment? The answer: My life was out of alignment. I was busy doing so many book signings and talks, and I chewed gum like a chain-smoker smoked. I needed to carve out a little more time for me, calm, relaxing solitude.

I started doing yoga weekly. I added a monthly massage. I threw out the gum. I went on a silent retreat. Within two weeks, my jaw was back in alignment. Within a month, the pain was gone and hasn't returned.

Judi Bar, a yoga therapist for the Cleveland Clinic Wellness Center and HeartLight Yoga, taught me how to listen to myself to discern what I should say yes to and no to in life. My radar was messed up. I needed clarity. I thought everything that came on my radar screen was mine to fix. I was saying yes to everything.

Judi had me sit in stillness for a few minutes. Erase every thought and just breathe, she suggested. Then she said, "Ask your body, What does a yes feel like? Let your body tell you what a yes feels like to you." So I sat still and asked. Nothing happened at first. Then I relaxed into the question and felt my face get warm until it felt like I was sitting in a sunbeam that warmed me all the way to my heart. I could feel a smile grow on my face and my chest expand wide with every breath as if my heart was opening up to the sun like a flower. Okay, that's a pretty good yes, she said.

Then she had me relax again and breathe deeply for a few minutes. "Now, ask your body, What does a no feel like?" So I asked. Nothing happened. It was blank. Then feelings of doubt and anxiety took over. I sat waiting to hear something loud and certain for a no. Instead, I felt a cloud of confusion settle over me and a trail wind of fear. Then my mind kicked up the chatter, that inner noise that always feels as irritating as static on the radio.

She asked me to describe my no. I didn't really feel one, I told her. "Tell me what you experienced," she said. I described the doubt, anxiety, noise, fear, and static.

"That is your no," she said. "When you experience that, you need to say no."

That moment changed my life. I always expected to feel with the clarity and certainty of a sledgehammer when I should say no. Since I didn't experience that powerful, clear no, I'd end up saying yes to every need and commitment. But I was saying yes to stuff that wasn't joyful, important, meaningful, or spiritual.

Now I listen to my body. I pause every hour and ask my body, *What do you need?* Then listen for the answer. It's amazing what I hear. My body actually needs to stop working to eat, pee, sleep, stretch, walk, drink, and move.

When I consult my soul, it says yes loud and clear. Yes is a fireworks display, or at least a sparkler of joy. And no? When my mind gets muddy or noisy and the clouds move in, that's my no.

When you learn to listen to yourself, it's amazing what you'll hear. You really do have the answers inside. Listen, and you'll discover when to say yes and, even better, when to say no.

Get in the game.

Where are the inspirational speakers when you need them most?

All the great commencement speeches delivered to graduating seniors should be replayed for incoming freshmen, whether they're entering college or high school. Freshman year is when new students really need to hear that great advice.

Hitch your wagon to a star.

March to the beat of a different drummer.

Take the road less traveled.

That freshman year is a rude awakening. Glory days? Not quite. The star falls. The drumstick breaks. The road dead-ends. Or it's littered with orange barrels and potholes.

There's a great Brad Paisley song where the country crooner sings the advice he'd give the teenager he used to be.

In the line "If I could write a letter to me," he's talking to the boy he was at 17. He'd tell that kid to take a typing class, study Spanish, and not worry so much about algebra.

What would I say to the student I used to be? It's the message I'd give every high school student: Get in the game. Try everything. Enjoy it all. Open your heart to someone and something to love, a girl, a boy, a subject, a sport. You don't have to merely endure those four years. You can make them as magical as you want by staying open to it all and attached to none of it.

As Theodore Roosevelt once said, "It's not the critic who counts: not the man who points out how the strong man stumbles or where the doer of deeds could have done better. The credit belongs to the man who is actually in the arena... who, at best, knows, in the end, the triumph of great achievement, and who, at the worst, if he fails, at least fails while daring greatly."

Dare to get in the game. Dare to dash into the arena of life.

That's what I'd like to tell all my friends' teenagers who are starting high school. I remember when my friends' children, Max, Kate, and Alex, were prenatal. Mere peanuts on ultrasound pictures. How can they now fill size 10 shoes? Tower over their parents? Play in the band at halftime?

If only I could convince them to enjoy it all. Even the worst moments will be the best stories to laugh over later in life, once you finish a few years of therapy.

But right now, it's all so serious.

Go easy on yourself. Some people love high school. Some people hate it. Either way, it only lasts four years. If you don't count summers, holidays, and weekends, it's really only two years out of your life.

Four years may seem like an eternity when you factor in writing a ten-page term paper for British literature, learning to drive, going on your first date, suffering your first broken heart, getting grounded for grades, constantly arguing with your parents, feeling like no one understands you, growing the largest zit on your nose an hour before prom, failing to make the cheerleading squad, getting hazed at band camp, or getting cut from the football team. So many things can go wrong and will.

Take the aerial view. Rise above it all and look down at the whole grand scheme that is your life. Those blue high school years? They're just a smidge of a gentle sky...or a treacherous lake. It all depends on your view, so it helps to maintain perspective.

Make good choices. As Dumbledore told Harry Potter, it is our choices that show what we truly are, far more than our abilities. Those choices, my friend, are all up to you. No one else. We're all dealt some bad cards in life. The difference is in how you play them. Or in how well you bluff.

Dab. The zits will go away faster if you don't squeeze them. A little skin tone cover-up works wonders. Wear wild socks, an outrageous shirt, or dye your hair a flaming orange to call attention elsewhere.

Give a little. Everyone says adolescents—I hate that word, too—are the most self-centered of all Homo sapiens. Prove them wrong. Lift a finger at home. Take out the trash. Run the vacuum. Clean out the garage. Reach out to a neighbor.

Hug your aunt Betty. Visit your uncle Joe. Every so often do one small thing to enhance someone else's life.

Join. Something. Anything. One club. One sport. One committee. One activity that makes your heart skip faster than a toddler's. Step away from the TV, cell phone, computer, and video games for a few hours. Try one new thing that you might like, not just something to please your parents or to get into the right college.

Lighten up. Everything feels like it's a big deal. It isn't. Or if it is, it'll shrink once you put your focus somewhere else.

Open up. Share your heart with someone who gets you, your humor, your music, your dreams. Don't date anyone who makes you miss out on the wonder of friends and family or you. Find someone who makes you smile, laugh, and float all the way home.

Be you. You are good enough. Your body will go wacky from hormones. Trust it anyway. Your heart will ride a wild roller coaster of emotions. Listen to it anyway. Don't trade away your body or your opinions or your values for someone else's cheap approval.

As the Paisley song says, don't be scared. These aren't even close to being the best years of your life.

It gets better. Trust me.

Better yet, trust you.

God doesn't always call the strong.
Sometimes you have to be weak
enough to serve.

We've all heard the stories.

Elvis Presley once got an F in music and was told to keep his day job driving trucks. Michael Jordan was cut from the high school basketball team. *Gone with the Wind* was rejected 38 times before it was published. J. K. Rowling lived on welfare before Harry Potter made her a billionaire.

Beethoven's music teacher said he was hopeless at composing. Winston Churchill flunked the Royal Military Academy entrance exam twice and finished last in his class. Lucille Ball got sent home from acting school for being too shy. Julia Roberts failed to get a part in the soap opera *All My Children*.

Thomas Edison was fired twice for not being productive enough. Babe Ruth held the record for most strikeouts. Walt Disney lost his job at a newspaper after he was told he lacked imagination. Van Gogh sold just one painting his whole life.

Abraham Lincoln suffered from depression, failed in two business ventures, and lost eight elections. Tell that to the Lincoln Memorial.

The failures of those great successes convince me that our weakness is often the flip side of our strength. I used to be terrified of speaking up. My career? Writing an opinion column for the largest newspaper in Ohio.

Our strengths and weaknesses are usually directly related. For the longest time I resisted embracing my strengths because to do so would make me confront my weaknesses. It was a long time before I learned that God can use both. It took me even longer to learn that sometimes God chooses us for our weaknesses, not for our strengths.

I find it a great comfort that, all through the Bible, God doesn't always choose the strong. He picks the flawed and the weak and transforms them. A person like Moses, who killed a man, is chosen to lead people from bondage to freedom. David, who ordered a man to be killed, is picked to be king. Then there's Jesus, who included among His 12 closest followers a man who lied to Him, a man who doubted Him, and a man who betrayed Him.

My favorite Christmas passage starts with "Fear not." Those two words mean God is going to do something powerful with someone weak. I love that moment in *A Charlie Brown Christmas* when Linus offers to explain the meaning of Christmas to his friend by quoting the Gospel of Luke:

Fear not: for, behold, I bring you good tidings of great joy, which shall be to all people. For unto you is born this day in the city of David a Savior, which is Christ the

Lord. And this shall be a sign unto you; ye shall find the babe wrapped in swaddling clothes, lying in a manger.

I've heard it said that we should read the Bible as if we are each of the characters in it. One year the priest at my church, Father Tom Fanta, gave a sermon as if he were the innkeeper who closed the door to the holy family on that first Christmas Eve. He acted the part from beginning to end, from his smug refusal to his shameful remorse.

He said that we are the innkeeper who shut the door and made no room for others. We're too busy to talk to that friend who is in the middle of a messy divorce. Our lives are too filled to make room for volunteering at a women's shelter or babysitting for a friend.

We are those shepherds, busy tending our sheep—our jobs, hobbies, families—and afraid when God comes to us, whether in the form of heavenly angels or earthly ones—friends, family, and strangers, or in the shape of problems and crises. We balk when called to go somewhere unfamiliar or somewhere undesired, some detour from our carefully constructed career paths or highly scheduled calendars.

We are like Joseph, who could have quietly left Mary instead of getting into a relationship that might demand more of him than he wanted to give. We prefer the normal, the steady, the predictable—something we can control. We plan our lives and in the planning are careful not to leave any room for God to come in and screw it all up.

We are like Mary, who, when first greeted by the angel, was scared. Would we really want God that close? "Fear not," the angel proclaimed.

What would happen if God called us to something higher? It sounds good—for a second. Until we count the cost. What if it means moving? Earning less money? Going back to school?

When God called Jeremiah, he wanted to decline; he claimed he was too young for the job. Moses wasn't so hot on being hired to corral the Israelites through the desert to the Promised Land.

A priest once told me he was unsure before his ordination whether he was strong enough to become a priest. Then someone asked him, "Are you weak enough?" Saying yes to God isn't about being strong, but about being weak and saying yes anyway.

Mother Teresa once said that she wasn't called to be successful; she was called to be faithful.

If your answer to the question "Are you strong enough to serve?" is no, maybe you're asking the wrong question.

Are you weak enough to serve?

When you have nothing but faith, you have enough.

All my life I had heard about third-world poverty. I had seen pictures of it in newspapers, on TV, and in magazines, but I'd never witnessed it firsthand until I went to El Salvador.

As the civil war there came to a close back in 1992, the editors at the *Beacon Journal* in Akron, Ohio, decided to send a reporter to write about the end of the war. A Salvadoran boy named José had lost his leg to a land mine and had received an artificial limb at a hospital near Akron. They wanted me to find him.

I headed to El Salvador with a photographer a week before the cease-fire was official. After one hour in El Salvador, my senses were numb. The sounds, the smells, the sights were overwhelming. People lived in huts made of dried mud and sticks. Roofs were sheets of cardboard or corrugated metal. The children were bone thin, dirty, barefoot, and begging by the roadside. Turkeys and chickens lived with people in their dirt-floor homes.

The drive from the airport to La Libertad was like a trip back in time. It seemed like a movie set. This couldn't be 1992. How could people live like this? We brought the latest in technology to transmit a story over the phone via computer in a country where you couldn't even drink the water.

The first night I stayed at a tiny motel with the newspaper photographer. The electricity went on and off. Bugs the size of birds flew in and out of the room. It was tough sleeping. The next night we stayed with the Cleveland missionary team in La Libertad. They showed us where soldiers and rebels killed people and dumped the bodies on the road. They pointed out bullet holes near the church altar. Someone shot a picture of Jesus through the shoulder during one shoot-out.

We slept on cots. We made sure the sheets didn't touch the floor and zipped our backpacks shut so tarantulas wouldn't crawl in. Bats flew in and out of the room. The sweet smell of mangoes and bananas in the market competed with manure from chickens, turkeys, and pigs. Garbage littered the street. Buses as loud as semitrucks woke us. Music blared from blocks away.

We hired an interpreter and went looking for José. The country is a virtual paradise of sea, sand, sky, mountains, volcanoes, and coconut trees. With the local priest's help, we found José living at the base of a volcano in Nejapa with his grandmother Eduarda Morales. He lived off a dirt road 50 miles from San Salvador. José was a quiet, broken boy who had lost both parents. Eduarda had lost nearly everyone she loved except José. They lived in a dried-mud hut smaller than a one-car garage. They shared a small wood slab of a bed. They had no electricity or running water.

Eduarda, who kept her silver hair tucked up in a bun, suffered from malaria, arthritis, and malnutrition. Her son was killed by soldiers, her grandson's leg blown off by a guerrilla land mine. She and the boy survived day to day, eating when they could find food or work. His mom had abandoned him shortly after he was born. His dad was shot to death in a field by soldiers.

José Raúl Morales was 11 going on 61. He had spent his whole life dodging soldiers' bullets. He lived in peace only once, when he was in Ohio for 12 weeks getting his artificial leg. The war was as much a part of his life as gathering sugarcane and grinding corn into supper. In Nejapa, 700 children died during the 12-year civil war. In the whole country, more than 75,000 died, huge for a country with five million people.

José was still scared to walk near the road where he lost his leg. He pointed to the tree where he was standing that morning in March 1988, when he was seven. Guerrillas had blown down the power lines. José was watching workers fix the power lines when he took one step back and heard the explosion.

The boy with him ran to get Eduarda. Soldiers rushed José to the hospital an hour away. Doctors amputated his leg above the knee. He was released three months later. José and two dozen other kids were airlifted to the United States to get medical care. He learned to use a prosthetic leg through a State Department program called Project HOPE, Health Opportunities for People Everywhere, which has since disbanded. He and Eduarda loved being in Ohio. The nurses and doctors spoiled them with gifts and love. People in the U.S. wanted to adopt him, but that would mean Eduarda would have to relinquish guardianship first. No one wanted that to happen.

José called his grandmother Mom. Eduarda was 74. As we walked through a field near her home, she told me how war happened everywhere, all around them. She pointed out where she first saw peace. How could peace have a spot?

"It was right here," she said, pointing a wrinkled finger to the bright blue sky where she saw firecrackers explode in celebration.

She didn't credit the rebels or the military for ending the war. She gave God all the credit.

"God gives us peace," she said. "We have to ask for it."

She never gave up asking. She had prayed for it every time she heard the shooting and bombs nearby. She prayed for it whenever the guerrillas invaded her home, when soldiers demanded food. She prayed for it as José hid under the bed or crouched in a corner.

She had no one but José. She sold whatever leftover coffee she could find in fields others had picked in. She worried that José one day wouldn't be able to work because of his missing leg. As a student he seldom missed school, even though he had to walk half a mile to fourth grade.

Every inch of her skin was wrinkled from 74 years in blazing sun. Her eyes and voice bore witness to a youthful spirit that neither poverty nor war could break. As the war turned José into a man, she kept the faith of a child.

"Whatever God wants," she said, nodding her head like an

obedient child. "I don't say anything because I can't. All I do is suffer with patience."

Somehow the gift of life itself was enough.

"Sí, sí!" she exclaimed. "After all that suffering, God has given me blessings. After all I have passed through, He still has me living. I give Him thanks."

Her prayer was, "Whatever God wills."

Eduarda gave thanks for life itself. Some days that was all she got.

I'd never seen a faith as rich as this poor woman's. She and José had nothing but each other and their faith. To her, that was everything. On that mountain, I was surrounded by the poorest people on earth, yet they possessed a faith richer than any I had ever experienced. They are faithful when they are starving, when they are homeless, when armies kill their loved ones, when guerrillas invade their homes, when land mines take their limbs. Through it all, they still praise God.

Until I met Eduarda, I never understood the beatitude "Blessed are the poor in spirit." The poor in spirit are blessed not because they are poor, not because they have nothing, but because they are attached to nothing but God.

When you have nothing to cling to but faith, you have enough.

Be a good monk.
Make your life a prayer.

The best writing mentor I ever had once studied to be a monk. Bill O'Connor didn't last long in the monastery, but he carried the experience with him into life.

We worked together as reporters at the *Beacon Journal* in Akron, Ohio. Whenever I got upset over small things or matters of great consequence that were actually of little consequence at all, he'd softly say, "Just be a good monk."

What did that mean? Did being a good monk mean vowing a life of poverty, chastity, and celibacy? Not to Bill. When I was scared about an upcoming deadline or dreaded some future event, Bill urged me to stay put in the present. When I was looking forward to an upcoming event and distracted by the future, Bill encouraged me to stay put in the present. Don't miss out on all the days between now and that hoped-for or dreaded event, he told me. Be present in the here and now.

Happiness isn't found seeking geographical cures for whatever ails you. The monks honored a vow of stability. They stayed in the monastery, even when they felt restless and irritable. The monks had a holy routine, a skeleton on which to wrap each day. They filled the sacred spaces with prayer whether they were washing dishes, baking bread, or chanting psalms.

Saint Benedict introduced the idea of making a commitment to remain in one community to keep the monks from wandering off in search of the perfect place to serve God, as if such a place existed. Outside the Abbey of Gethsemani in Kentucky where Trappist monk Thomas Merton lived, two simple words engraved in stone over the metal gates both greet you and haunt you when you pass by: GOD ALONE.

That's the solution to every problem. More God. So many of us, myself included, try to fill the God-size hole with everything else. Booze, drugs, chocolate, donuts, dating, gambling, sex, shopping, winning, and the endless affirmation of others. No matter what we put in that place, we still feel empty because nothing fits in that hole but God.

Merton ended up spending his life in that Kentucky monastery writing volumes on the holiness in the ordinary life around him. You don't have to be a monk to realize that the search for happiness takes place on the inner landscape, not by changing homes or careers or marriages.

In my quest for more God, I've visited the Abbey of Gethsemani. If you want to pray nonstop, you are welcome to participate in the list of weekday worship, from Vigils at 3:15 a.m. to Compline at 7:30 p.m. In between, the monks pray the psalms and work.

I woke for all of those, even though my head nodded off during the chanting. I met Brother Matthew Kelty, who used to give sermons right after dinner. He told us, "He is a whimsical God." This from a monk who has been known to wear cowboy boots under his robe.

Up on the hill, I sat in an Adirondack chair next to a giant statue and recalled the voice of an old Amish man who used to tell everyone he'd meet, "Pray for a grateful, humble heart." In the cemetery, every monk has the same humble cross. A short white one with clover-leaf rounded sides and a tiny plaque with a name engraved and their date of death. They look like strange white lilies planted on the green slope.

Four days at Gethsemani taught me that I can live without newspapers and telephones and televisions. I can live in silence, but I did end up talking to myself quite a bit. I can live without ice cream and chocolate, but the craving for them remains.

The monks can point the way to God, but it is in the arms of my husband, daughter, and stepsons that God lives and breathes and dwells in me. I came seeking and realized I had already found it. Click your red ruby slippers. There's no place like the home God has already created in your heart. I possessed the power all along. The presence of God is already in me.

My friend Father Jim Lewis is fond of offering this advice to everyone he counsels: God is the answer. Now what was your question?

I've never forgotten a simple story a man shared with a group of my friends about Catholic school. Michael was having a bad day and spit on a nun. A nun! That's like a felony in Catholic school. She hauled him off to the principal's office.

He sat outside the principal's door for what seemed like days. He wondered what hell would be his punishment. Then the nun came by and sat down next to him. He expected her to be harsh. Instead, she said ever so gently, "Michael, make your life a prayer." He never forgot it.

Make your life a prayer. Not a quest for more achievements, awards, popularity, power, praise, money, or fame.

For many, prayer is something you say in a crisis. We all have our favorite 911 calls to God. You can pray in a pinch or you can make your whole life a prayer. For me, cancer came along and did both. It made me say crisis prayers to survive and it led me to see my whole life as a prayer, as a gift for others. Every day I plug into God, into my power source, so I stay Higher Powered all day.

How do you make your life a prayer? Practice.

Every day I bless my life with words by Saint Augustine, who called upon the help of the Holy Spirit to transform him. Others might refer to that same aspect of God as Spirit, Divine Love, Eternal Presence, whatever works for you. Augustine's words work for me:

Breathe into me, Holy Spirit, that all my thoughts may be holy.
Move into me, Holy Spirit, that my work, too, may be holy.
Attract my heart, Holy Spirit, that I may love only what is holy.
Strengthen me, Holy Spirit, that I may defend what is holy.
Protect me, Holy Spirit, that I may always be holy.

Then I breathe. All day long when my mind starts to whirl, I pause. *Just breathe,* I remind myself.

Sometimes I stop and bless myself, place my hands on my head, and ask God to bless what I think. Then I cover my ears and ask God to bless what I hear. Then I touch my eyes and pray for God to bless what I see. Then I place my hand on my mouth and ask God to bless what I say. Then I rest my hand on my heart and ask God to bless what I feel. Finally, I hold open both hands and ask God to bless what I do.

Then I move into the day, knowing I'm covered, and so are all the people I meet.

Believe in abundance.

The call came into the newsroom a few weeks before Christmas, a call that would forever open my mind and heart to believe in abundance.

Christmas is a time when hearts are a little more open to miracles. It's also a time when newspapers are flooded with pleas from people wanting help. There are so many needy people and so many worthy causes, you don't know where to start, or if you do, you don't know where to end. How many people can you help? How much can you help each one? As a journalist, if you write too many stories about the need for food, shelter, clothing, and toys, you risk burning readers out. How many times can you go to the same well and ask people to dip into their wallets to help another stranger?

By the time Staci Callihan's family called me that December, my own heart felt a bit fatigued from all the need.

Staci's aunt wanted a reporter to write about her niece, who was in the intensive-care unit at Akron Children's Hospital. Staci was five years old and had so many things wrong with her she'd never leave the hospital to go home unless someone could transform her home into a virtual medical center.

The little girl was on a respirator. The only way doctors would allow her to come home would be if she had a new bedroom with special air-conditioning, a filtered furnace, and space for a breathing apparatus, monitors, and a wheelchair to pass through the house. The home would need a wheelchair ramp and a new room added to meet all of Staci's needs. Even the wiring had to be updated to handle all the medical machines. Her parents couldn't afford it.

Her mother, Lily, quit her job to be with Staci. Her dad, Jess, earned less than $25,000 a year. By the time her aunt finished reading off the list of what Staci needed, I was numb.

I almost turned her down. The need was so huge, even if I wrote about her situation, who would be able to respond? Who could donate the thousands of dollars it would take? I tried to tell the woman I couldn't help her. Staci was going to die anyway, and it could be in a matter of weeks or months. I didn't want to give her any false hope. It would be awful to write about her and have no one come forward to help.

Just come visit her, the aunt begged. Just come meet her, she pleaded. To her, I was the media. I was her last resort, her only hope. I couldn't imagine anyone would help the family, but a tiny spark of faith inside me said, *You never know.*

Doctors had urged the family to let the little girl die, which made the request seem even more outrageous. All I could see was how much money it would take to make all those changes to the house. What I couldn't see was how much her sister, Rachael, wanted her home. I couldn't see how much her parents loved their sleeping beauty.

When I met Staci, she looked like a life-size doll. She wore a glittery clip with stars in her brown silky hair. She had the longest, darkest eyelashes. She wore a powder-blue dress with white tights and shiny patent leather shoes. A stuffed Santa sat in her crib and a plastic Christmas tree sat on a monitor while "Silent Night" played on the radio. Staci slept through it all. Her mother called her Sleeping Beauty. All Staci did was sleep. The cerebral palsy, pneumonia, seizures, and breathing problems had worn out her tiny body. Tubes ran in and out of her nose and mouth. She should have been sitting on Santa's lap, playing with dolls, wondering if reindeer could fly. Instead, she was fighting for her life.

A neurologist said Staci wouldn't live to be ten. Lily knew that Staci's life would be brief, but she wanted her daughter to live what was left of it at home.

"She wasn't meant to live long, but she's here for a special reason," her mother said. "She's like an angel from heaven."

How could I say no to an angel at Christmas?

So I wrote the story detailing the little girl's need. Part of me felt awful giving her family false hope and asking readers for so much at a time when family budgets were stretched thin. I doubted the story would even bring the Callihan family enough money for a wheelchair ramp.

The call came into the newsroom the day after I wrote

about Staci. The owner of a construction company read the article in the *Beacon Journal* and wanted to help. Paul Testa of P. J. Testa Builders Inc. had already spoken to the Callihans.

"I'll build it," he told me.

The wheelchair ramp?

"The whole thing," he said.

He had already talked to all his suppliers, subcontractors, and laborers. They all agreed to donate their time, equipment, parts, and skills. He pulled together a team to build that extra room and make all the renovations on the house. For free.

The Christmas gift to Staci exceeded $20,000.

It didn't matter to Paul and the others that Staci could die any day. One of his workers had told him, "If she's home for a day, it's worth it."

Paul told me that he came forward to do the job, to do it all, because he knew no one else would have the resources to do it. And because it was Christmas.

Staci got to come home for more than a day. She lived there for ten months. She almost lived to see another Christmas. She died in her new bedroom while her mother was out Christmas shopping.

Lily donated all of Staci's gifts to their church so other needy families would have presents to open.

"It makes me grateful that she died at home," Lily said. "She was always happy here."

Staci was buried on December 22, 1993, a year to the day that Paul Testa and the crew first came out to her home in Akron to start building that room. When I saw Staci's photo on the obituary page, it hit me that this special-needs child had fulfilled a special need. Staci Callihan taught me to never underestimate the capacity of the human heart, to never doubt how large it can expand.

She taught me that no wish is too much to ask for. No need is too great to meet. No miracle is too absurd to hope for. And no life is too short to have meaning.

*Shine your light, no matter how dark
the world around you appears.*

When the lights went out, the first thing we thought was
terrorist attack.

We soon found out it was a blackout. Not just in Cleveland,
but most of the East Coast, Midwest, and parts of Canada.
That dark day became one of the brightest in our lives.

My friend's son, Finnegan, discovered light during the biggest blackout in U.S. history. The 18-month-old ran around
our kitchen in the dark wearing nothing but a diaper and a
grin, his chubby cheeks aglow from the flashlight he crammed
in his mouth. He held it to his face and pranced from room to
room like a giant lightning bug.

He won't remember a thing about the blackout, only what
we tell him.

If we're honest, we'll tell him that at first we feared that
terrorists had crippled the country by wiping out our power,

since the biggest blackout in U.S. history happened on August 14, 2003, just two years after the 9/11 attack. We'll tell him that once we got over the queasy "What's next?" feeling, the blackout really wasn't so bad.

Some 55 million of us went without power, including most of New York City, Baltimore, Buffalo, Detroit, Cleveland, and Toronto. Trains shut down in Pennsylvania. Airports closed down and became campsites for stranded travelers. Times Square billboards went dark. Broadway shows were canceled. Subways came to a halt and thousands had to be evacuated.

The outage left us without power, so we created our own power surge.

We drove home during rush hour with no traffic lights to protect us from road hogs. Guys in shorts and baseball caps directed cars, conducting a symphony with no horn section. No drivers got angry enough to hit theirs as the self-deputized waved their arms to and fro, directing the flow. Every intersection became a four-way stop with people politely taking turns.

We'll tell him that being "on the grid" meant that people got trapped in elevators, that shopping malls closed, meat spoiled, ice cream melted, that blacked-out electronic eyes kept public restroom sinks from flowing and toilets from flushing at airports where planes couldn't fly.

We'll tell him how he and his mom had a slumber party in our living room because their fourth-floor apartment was too hot in the 90-degree heat without any air-conditioning or fans, and it was safer and more fun to get through a crisis together.

We'll tell him that while we ate by candlelight, old folks sat in lawn chairs outside senior high-rises, neighbors sat on stoops and chatted, people conversed by candlelight on porches, and children stared up at stars normally extinguished by streetlights.

We'll tell him how a desperate crowd ignored the two red CLOSED signs outside a Walgreen's drugstore, how 40 people waited for batteries, water, candles, and ice, but no one barked at employees who let in only two at a time. We'll tell him how the people at the front of the line danced and moms at the back of the line promised their kids ice cream for dinner. We'll tell him that no one got irate when one man left with ten gallons of water and the last of the ice. Instead, the crowd applauded, a stranger yelled out, "Mission accomplished!" and everyone smiled.

We'll tell him how we came home and discovered that we couldn't open the garage door, see the food in the fridge, retrieve phone messages, or microwave dinner.

We'll tell him that no matter how advanced the world gets, we should always carry cash; keep matches, candles, batteries, bottled water, canned food, and a battery-operated radio in the house; never let the gas tank drop below half; and always know your neighbors by name.

We'll brag about how we couldn't use an ATM, play a CD, pop in a DVD, use our computers, or watch CNN. We'll tell him how cell phone service was interrupted from the overload of calls and most phones went dead because no one could recharge them.

We'll describe how we had to boil water and sniff our food; that we couldn't tell whether we were getting cleaner or dirtier when we showered because the water was yellow to start with.

We'll reminisce about how nice it was to take a break from reading e-mail, surfing the Web, and watching reality TV to get to know the real people next door and across the street and listen to crickets with the windows open and run around catching fireflies.

We'll tell him that all over New York City, Toronto, Detroit, and Cleveland, hardly anyone looted, that stores gave shoes to people who had to walk miles to get home, strangers offered rides to other strangers, people held tailgate parties by the curb, grocers grilled hot dogs in the streets, stores gave away ice cream, and neighborhoods held all-night blackout block parties.

We'll tell him that when the power failed us, we didn't fail each other.

Plato once said: "We can easily forgive a child who is afraid of the dark; the real tragedy of life is when men are afraid of the light."

On one of the darkest days in history, we embraced the light that we all became in the darkness.

*Comfort the sick. When everyone
else flees, be the one who stays.*

When I was going through cancer, I tried to keep my life
as normal as possible. Right after I finished one of my last chemotherapy treatments, I headed off to speak at a journalism
conference as the president of the National Society of Newspaper Columnists.

I tried to look as perky as possible on that flight from Cleveland to San Diego, but I felt pretty awful. The flight attendant
looked crestfallen when she saw me, bald, thin, and weak,
curled up in the seat.

"You're my hero," she told me as she handed me a pile of
pillows. I think she figured it was my Make-A-Wish trip. Geez,
did I look that bad?

Probably.

Did it help to know it?

Not really.

What do you say to people who have cancer? Anyone who has had the disease gets asked that. Right now there are ten million Americans alive who have had cancer. As baby boomers age, there will be even more diagnosed and living with cancer. Cancer isn't the death sentence it used to be, but so many people think it still is.

I've always wanted to give people a cheat sheet with the basics. The American Cancer Society offers endless tips online at www.cancer.org. The agency's best advice? Respond from the heart.

My best advice? Let's start with what not to do. I learned these tips from having cancer and from supporting friends and family members who have had cancer. Everyone is different, but here's a general list on how to comfort the sick that can be applied to other illnesses as well:

Don't flee. Cancer brings out the best and the worst in people. When it came to friends, cancer separated the weak from the strong. Some didn't make the cut. Some friends go AWOL. One of my dearest friendships didn't survive cancer. She couldn't bear to see me sick. We used to talk every day. Once I got cancer, she stopped calling and didn't return my calls. Don't be that friend who leaves. Write, visit, e-mail, text, call. Stay involved for the long haul. The longer the treatment lasts, the lonelier it gets.

Don't share horror stories about people who didn't make it. Too many people want to tell long, drawn-out stories with bad endings. If the main character of your story dies, that's not considered a happy ending. It's not helpful.

When it comes to cancer, there are no right words. Keep it simple and say, "I'm here for you," and mean it. Sometimes no words are best. Your presence alone matters more than anything you can say. Keep in touch, even when the patient is too tired to talk, even if he or she falls asleep every time you visit, cancels plans, and doesn't return calls. Continue to be there. Their number one priority is getting well, not returning your call or casserole dish or writing a thank-you.

Don't offer medical advice or discourage the person from pursuing the course of treatment he or she has chosen. Whether you agree with them or not, respect the choices they have made. You aren't the oncologist.

Don't overreact and jump from diagnosis to death. The person in front of you is very much alive, no matter what the prognosis.

Don't blame the person for being sick. Don't point out that it might be from lack of exercise, smoking, too much red meat, or negative thinking.

Don't point out anything that isn't flattering, like how big someone's ears look when they're bald from chemo. When my hair started growing back, it poked straight up like brown peach fuzz. One woman told me my new hair looked like dirt. Ouch. Make sure your words are necessary, helpful, or kind.

Don't be afraid of the person. Cancer isn't contagious. Don't stand ten feet away if you've always been a hugger. Get in there and hug.

Don't say you know how the person feels. You really don't. Even if you've had cancer, you don't know how this person feels with cancer.

Don't ask personal questions that only doctors and spouses are allowed to ask. Allow the person some privacy.

Some people want to keep their medical situations private. Others go public. Each person has the right to keep quiet or shout it from the rooftops.

Don't promise to do something you can't or won't do. Offer only what you are willing to follow through on.

Don't take anything personally. Cancer can make a person irritated, tense, sad, depressed, and angry. It also makes a person awfully tired. The patient might not always call back. Keep offering. Remember, the burden of friendship is on the well person.

Don't rush the person to talk about something she isn't ready to discuss. After my friend Monica ended up in hospice care, she still talked about getting the next chemo treatments. We knew there weren't going to be any more, but we allowed her to hope. We didn't have to remind her that she was dying. She was 39. She still wanted to marry and have children one day. We listened and encouraged her to relax while she got her energy back. She never did, but she was able to savor every meal, every visitor, every ray of sunshine coming into her room before she died.

When you find out someone has cancer, hold the gasps. They're still among the living. Simply ask, "What can I do to be most helpful?" Then listen for an answer.

Now for the dos.

Do stay in touch by phone, e-mail, and cards. Allow the person to respond as energy allows.

Instead of asking "What can I do?" offer a few specifics. When you throw out choices, it makes it easier to just grab one when your brain is fuzzy from chemo. Ask: May I drive you to the library? Take you to a movie? Get you a milk shake?

Send movies, books, gift baskets, flowers, and meals in containers the person doesn't have to return. Order three months' worth of Netflix. When Monica was in the hospital, her sister Jacqui made a list of 100 top movies to watch. They made their way through the list and I supplied a few months of Netflix. Give gift certificates to local restaurants and pizza parlors.

Help the main caregiver, too. Give the caregiver a chance to go for a walk, take a nap, and talk about something besides cancer. Set up a plan for a food corps to drop off meals. Help set up a CaringBridge website, e-mail Listserv, or a blog to communicate easily to masses of people with little effort.

It's hard to ask for help. Make it easy for them. Offer to run errands. Watch the kids. Bring over a meal. Hire a maid service to help out. Do the laundry. Fill the fridge. If you can't do something you are asked to do, be honest.

Strangers, friends, and family held me up. They dropped off mail from work and watched movies with me. They sent so many flower arrangements the living room looked like a funeral home. My friend Judy stayed with me after the surgery and washed my hair in the kitchen sink the first two days when I wasn't allowed to shower. Jane bought me a nightgown and robe. Sheryl brought me lunch, boosted my spirits, and updated me so I never fell behind on the latest gossip at work. Beth brought me stacks of movies from the library.

So many people offered support that I had to organize them into battalions. Jim, a coworker who lost his sister, Pat, to cancer, gave me a copy of the journal she kept during her battle. Pat created her own healing corporation. She appointed a Director of Spirituality, a Director of Humor, a Director of

Beauty, a Chief Waitress, and a Head Shaver. The goal of each was to run various teams to help her get better.

It inspired me to write down the names of everyone who offered help. They all said, "If there's anything I can do for you, let me know." I divided everyone into groups. Those who could cook and clean would be my caregivers. Those who were always optimistic about life would form my cheering section. Those who made me laugh through a lifetime of bad relationships became the Humor Committee. The Beauty Committee could pencil in eyebrows once mine fell out, pick out the right earrings to soften the glare of my bald head, and show me how to tie a scarf.

I put my husband in charge of billing and insurance so I didn't have to look at a hospital bill and worry about the cost of getting well. I've heard of others who appointed people to gather the latest medical info, keep records organized, jot down medicines taken and side effects, and go with people to their treatments.

Help the person with cancer delegate duties so no one gets worn out. Make a list of what they need and want, then make a list of family, friends, coworkers, neighbors who might be the best matches to meet those needs and wants. The transportation committee can organize rides, cover parking expenses for family visits to the hospital, and carpools for soccer games. The spiritual team can offer Reiki, meditation, prayer, yoga, journaling, prayer, music therapy, tapes to listen to, or inspirational books on tape.

Listen. You don't have to give answers or advice or offer a plan of action. Just listen. Get comfortable with silence and always look the person in the eye no matter how they look.

Allow them to talk about other things besides cancer: movies, books, current events. They aren't just a patient. They are still your mother, father, sister, brother, friend, coworker.

Listen with your heart, not just your ears. They aren't asking you to fix cancer; they just want to know you're with them in the midst of it. Be an outlet. Let the person cry, swear, whine, and complain without any judgment.

If you feel uncomfortable, make peace with discomfort. The person with cancer is feeling much more uncomfortable than you are. Try to see it through their eyes. Look past the monitors, the IV, the scars, the bald head, and remember the person you love is still the same.

When in doubt, just ask, "Is there anything I can do to make you more comfortable?" Then do it.

Good advice for flight attendants, too.

You have an endless supply of abundance from a wealthy Father who loves you, and so does everyone else.

My dad's biggest lesson about money centered upon how to fold it.

If you reached into your pocket and pulled out a crumpled dollar bill, or worse, a wad of bills crushed into a ball, Dad shook his head and said, "That's no way to treat your money."

Then he'd carefully iron it out with his big calloused hands, those hands tanned by working in the sun hammering shingles and hanging spouting, those hands stained by tar and Rust-Oleum, those hands scarred by cuts from heating ducts and furnaces.

Dad taught us to carry our money pressed flat, folded in half longwise first, then folded in half sideways. That way, when you tucked it in your pocket, if it opened up it would get stuck and never fall out.

My dad respected money because he had so little of it

growing up. His family lost everything in the Great Depression. He quit school in the eighth grade so he could work to help his parents and siblings. My dad spent his life as a sheetmetal worker. In summers, he worked on roofs. In winter, he repaired furnaces. In between, he made heating ducts for businesses.

I never knew how much he earned. My mom got an allowance from him to buy groceries and things for the house. When my dad lost his job, she got a part-time job and the shame of it nearly killed him. It broke something in him to see his wife work. He wanted his 11 children to stay in the small town we were raised in. He felt hurt when we all moved away to go to college or to pursue careers.

Like many folks who grew up blue-collar, we didn't think much of rich people. Growing up, we felt it was okay to look down our noses on people who had lots of money. We weren't allowed to harbor prejudices about anyone else. We were taught that people of all races, nationalities, and religions were to be respected. But people with money were "those people."

No one actually said they were bad people, but some subliminal message told us that wealth and greed were sinful partners. Being rich wasn't something to admire or aspire to.

In a strange way, we almost glorified poverty. "Blessed are the poor in spirit" became "Blessed are the poor." We were taught in Catholic church that Jesus was poor, as if that should be our highest goal in life, to be poor.

It took me a long time to learn that God has nothing against money and nothing against people who have a lot of it. Growing up, whenever someone else benefited from a lottery win, an inheritance, or a big raise, I heard people warn, "Money is the root of all evil," as if it were a curse. That's not what it says in the Bible. It says, "The love of money is the root of all evil."

It took a lot of work for me to stop glorifying poverty and demonizing wealth. I wasn't going to have a rich life by doing that. My mind-set, not my wallet, kept me stuck and limited my earning potential and my ability to give to others. I spent many years avoiding money. I didn't invest in retirement. I couldn't summon the courage to ask for a raise. I had enough to get by and tried to be grateful for that.

I've heard it said that money problems are never about money. The problem is how you think about money or how you behave with your money. The problem is your relationship with money. We all have one. Is it a good relationship or a bad one?

One day my friend Vicki lent me her copy of *Think and Grow Rich*. The title seemed almost pornographic. The word *rich* turned me off. Was it really okay to think about growing rich? I read the book but resisted that word *rich*. To want to be rich seemed a betrayal of my dad's blue-collar roots and steel-toed work boots.

Over time I read other books about finances. Most of them suggested examining where your attitudes about money came from. Almost all of mine came from my dad. My dad taught me, "Money doesn't grow on trees." When we wanted any-thing, his response was always, "You don't need it." When we complained about wanting something better, he'd scold us, "A blind man would be happy to see it."

My mom had no income most of her life. One day I came home from a girlfriend's house and was so excited to tell my mom that my friend had a stained-glass window in her home.

A stained-glass window! My mom snapped, "Isn't our house good enough?" Maybe she was having a rough day, but the message I heard was, Don't admire what you don't have. Be happy with what you have. Period.

My parents had a poverty consciousness that was hard to shed. Childhoods shaped by the Great Depression left them both with a constant fear of not having enough.

We wore hand-me-downs. Dad never bought on credit. He paid cash for everything. He came from a generation of workaholics, providers who spent the day working, came home, read the paper, ate dinner, then went to the garage and worked some more. My dad's only hobby was work.

Having fun was seen as being lazy. Play was a waste of time. The goal was to have a steady job and security. To take bold risks and go after what you loved in life was irresponsible.

A poverty consciousness believes in limits and competition, scarcity and lack, fear and shame. You grab, clasp, and tighten your grip on what little you have and can't imagine releasing it for something better.

I used to be afraid of getting a six-figure salary. That would mean I was wealthy, which would be wrong, so I refused to ask for a raise. I used to admire a car on concrete blocks with doors that didn't match more than I admired a shiny new BMW, Mercedes, or Porsche. I used to see cutting coupons as an act of nobility.

I constantly said things like, "I can't. I don't have the money. I can't afford it."

It took a long time for me to let go of that poverty mentality, to realize that my financial destiny is up to me, that it isn't genetic, that it isn't locked in for life.

I started believing that there is enough to go around, for me and for everyone. I started believing in a God of abundance, a God of prosperity. My money is God's money, and God has nothing against money.

When you change how you think about money, your income will change. When I let go of my poverty mentality, my capacity to receive and give changed. It took work. I wrote down a whole list of new messages to tell myself about money and abundance and wealth.

I keep an abundance journal where I write down signs of abundance, the people, places, and moments that fill my heart and the people whose hearts I fill with blessings, gifts, praise, and kind deeds. I'll jot down the lunch my daughter treats me to, the meals I cook for others, hugs given and received, coins found on the sidewalk, writing awards won, extra tips given to waitresses, calls, cards, pep talks, and positive e-mails sent and received, thank-you notes from nieces and nephews.

I bless every check I write. Instead of grumbling and griping about the gas bill, the electric bill, and the water bill, I give thanks for a warm house, lights to read by, hot showers, and cold food. I wrote the word *abundance* in bright red letters and taped it onto the container that stores my bills and checkbook.

I created an abundance team of people in my life who want the best for me even more than I do. I run my money decisions by them and share my victories.

I practice giving joyfully. When it comes to paying taxes, I don't complain. It's proof that I had an abundant year. No more whining as if I'm the victim of the government. My tax dollars cover all those gifts I enjoy: a fully stocked library, paved highways, police and fire protection, and schools that educate all the children in my community.

I wrote out the salary of my dreams on a fake check from the universe and taped it to the medicine cabinet to look at every time I open the door. I look in the mirror and tell myself, "Regina, you are worthy of abundance." I stay open and ready to receive it.

A prosperity consciousness doesn't mean some people win big and others lose. It's a win-win. It's believing there is more than enough for everybody. It's about financial freedom. It's about having faith. It's about mindful spending, saving, and giving. It's about loving what you do so much that you never work a day in your life.

I consciously welcome money into my life. I view money as a positive thing that can see me through retirement so I'll never be a burden on my children. It will bless their lives long after I'm gone. I can do good deeds with money now and bless the world.

God is the Source in my life. The boss, the company, the economy don't rule my life. Instead of saying, "I can't afford that" I now pause and ask myself, *Do I really want to afford that? If so, how can I?*

I no longer look down on money. I look within for abundance.

I no longer look down on the rich. I see myself as rich.

I have an endless supply of abundance from a wealthy God who loves me.

So do you.

Carry as you climb.

Some people step into your life and leave an imprint on your heart, one that never goes away.

You recall the precise moment you met. Monica Turoczy was one of them.

I met her a few years ago at a fund-raiser for the Cleveland Rape Crisis Center. She wasn't the tallest woman in the room, but she looked it because she held her head higher than everyone. Her black hair was always perfectly styled; her lipstick matched her fingernails, purse, and shoes.

She was networking up a storm, chatting to everyone in the room, making everyone else feel important. She knew that people love to talk about themselves, so she looked you in the eye, asked a million questions, and actually wanted to hear the answers.

From the moment we met, we became friends. She always

greeted me with two words, "Hey, doll." And she always sprinkled her favorite F word in every conversation: *fantastic.*

She was 15 years younger than me but always acted like a big sister looking out for me, giving me advice on fashion, work, and relationships. My friend Monica lived by the motto "Carry as you climb."

Whatever career ladder you're headed up, take someone with you. You can climb a career ladder in heels, steel-toed work boots, or a pair of Hush Puppies. It doesn't matter what you wear; it matters who you carry up the ladder with you. Value each person you meet, no matter what his or her position is in the organization.

No one should climb the career ladder alone. Carry someone else up as you make the ascent. "Don't ever run away from the fact that you're a woman in business," Monica told younger women. "It's the one advantage you hold in a roomful of gentlemen. Too many women think they need to network the way men do. Make your own mold."

She worked and networked with passion, because it was never just for her, it was always about enriching the lives of others. Monica empowered women to be their best selves. Instead of learning about baseball and golf to be one of the boys, she invented a schmoozing event for the girls. She created the Power Pedi, where businesswomen networked while getting pedicures. She invited a mix of powerful women, young and old, veterans and rookies, to talk business during pedicures.

"If men can blow off the afternoon for golf, we can blow it off for pedicures," she told me.

Her philosophy? "Find your groove and ride it like a wave."

That wave took her to Washington, D.C., after she left her job at the Northeast Ohio Council on Higher Education. Then one day in May, I ran into her aunt at Costco.

"Did you hear about Monica?" she asked. "She's having brain surgery tomorrow."

It started as a headache that wouldn't go away. The scans showed cancer everywhere, in her brain, lungs, and abdomen. Monica went from a vibrant woman of 38 to a dying woman with stage IV cancer.

She moved back to Cleveland to get the best medical care in the world. Her mom had died years before from breast cancer, so Monica's sister, Jacqui, took over the job of mothering Monica every step of the way.

They fought the good fight. Surgery. Radiation. Chemotherapy. Jacqui camped out at the foot of Monica's bed at University Hospital for weeks. She carried her sister, sometimes literally, helping her learn to walk again when the cancer wrapped around her spine.

I'll never forget how Monica dressed for her first chemotherapy. She came in dressed for a date. I wore jeans and sneakers to my chemo appointments. Monica wore a gauzy white skirt with a bright pink blouse that matched her shoes, fingernails, and snappy hat.

When the brain surgery left her woozy, she asked, "So what's shaking with you?" When the brain radiation left her forgetful, she'd say, "So tell me what you were just talking about." When the brain cancer left her dying, she'd say, "So how is that grandson of yours?"

I felt bad that I kept promising her it would get better. My friend Patrick, who is a priest, gently reminded me, "It did."

At the funeral, Jacqui asked me to read a poem Monica wrote about herself. It was actually a personal ad she had written. It described Monica better than I ever could:

I am a snappy pair of black patent leather knee boots. I am a great book and a hot latte on a cold, sunny D.C. morning on the Potomac. I am a fresh, cherry-red mani/pedi in strappy new sandals in the springtime.

I am the gal who will always gaze with wonder and delight at the approach from the Parkway on a full moon night, with the dome and the Washington Monument draped in light.

I am an afternoon at the Renwick followed by scotch and steaks at Charlie Palmer's.

I am a smartass . . . witty and funny.

I am a round of 18 scoring about 90 on a sunny day in Hilton Head or at Congressional or wishing I was in Augusta in April.

I am a wine which sells better at a tasting than from a catalog. I am the "snap-crackle-pop" on your mind as you begin your third conference call late Friday afternoon.

I am the toe-to-toe debater equal to the match on unions, foreign policy, education, health care, and the midterms.

I am happy like Christmas morning as the cherry blossoms open to the first sunshine of April along the Basin, with Thomas Jefferson looking on.

I am the date simply thrilled with a stroll through the falls at the FDR and a cheese pizza at Paradiso.

I am barefoot on the beaches at Porto Mari in the middle of February sipping tamarind juice after snorkeling with the clown fish.

I am the sunshine which lives only in the hills north of Siena, bouncing off the Chianti hills and the green olive groves.

I am the flame you don't fear.

Monica was a human sparkler. She burned bright and fast, then *poof!* she was gone. But her light will burn on forever in all the people she carried.

Be an original. Forge your own path.

The best graduation speeches are short. Few people remember long speeches. The Gettysburg Address was two minutes long. The other guy who talked for two hours? Few remember the message Edward Everett gave that day.

Lincoln was either humble or naive to say, "The world will little note, nor long remember what we say here; while it can never forget what they did here." We've never forgotten those words posted next to his monument in Washington, D.C., that end with "that government of the people, by the people, for the people shall not perish from the earth."

I don't remember who spoke at my high school graduation or my two college graduations. I've given a commencement address to a high school, to a college, and to a police academy. When I consulted what other great speakers had said, most of them urged graduates to follow their own path, quoting

Henry David Thoreau, who wrote about marching to the beat of a different drummer.

How do you follow your own path?

You let life prune you. The job you don't want could lead to the career you do want. The lover you longed for but who didn't stick around may enable you to find the perfect mate at the next dinner party. Rejection is a necessary part of the pruning process. Before I graduated from college, I sent out 30 résumés and got 30 rejection letters back. The painful process of elimination led me to the only door left open, the journalism job at a small paper that jump-started my career.

Never say never. The job you don't want could lead to the career you do want.

I told myself I'd never write government news and business news. Too boring, too stiff, too dry. My first job? Covering city hall for the *Lorain Journal* in Lorain, Ohio. My next job? Covering business for the *Beacon Journal* in Akron. Wrong job, but the right place.

Expand the box. Instead of waiting for your boss to give you a title and job description, give yourself your own title and grow into it. Don't say, "I'm just a (fill in the blank)." Act as if you are more. Meet your boss's agenda first, but always meet your agenda, too. Rather than wait for your new lover to say "I love you" first, why don't you take the chance? Take risks and love first.

Love the work in progress that you are right now: You aren't a finished product. You are constantly evolving. Honor the great design of the Master. Uncover the blueprint of your soul. Be creative. Daring. Outlandish. Outrageous. Be an original. Be you. I remember hearing about a man who was so enamored by the work of Mother Teresa that he wrote her often about coming to Calcutta to make her work his life's work. One day he finally got a letter back. Her words stunned him: "Find your own Calcutta."

Create your own map. Instead of finding your place in the world, design one. Don't use someone else's map. The problem with maps (besides the fact that you can never fold them back up) is that they will only take you to where someone else has already been. That's why there is no map for the rest of your life. Plus, maps are too conservative. There are no exclamation points on a map.

Don't go to Notre Dame just because everyone in your family went there if your heart is set on Georgetown. Don't go to college if your real dream is to work on the railroad and you've heard that whistle blowing in your heart ever since you were a child. Don't stay in the small town you grew up in and work at your family's business if your heart's desire is to be onstage in New York or in a director's chair in Hollywood.

When you run out of map, use a compass. We each have one. It's inside of you. It points to your true north, the place designed for you alone, to your heart's desire, to that spot God designed for you alone. Consult it whenever you feel lost.

Listen to yourself. Silence the voices all around you. People will come by and shake the snow globe that is your world. A critical comment, some idle gossip, a slammed door, and the snow starts swirling. Be calm, be quiet. Let it all swirl. It will all settle and you'll discover that the treasure inside remains steadfast and strong.

There's a true place for everyone. Yours doesn't belong to anyone else.

For many, the hardest part of life begins after the commencement ceremony ends. The tassels have been turned, the caps tossed, the speeches forgotten. You're soon on your own in the world of graduate school, work, travel, or military service. For a while, you might feel confident with your choice, even boast about it. But one day you could find yourself wondering, *What the hell did I do?*

It could be the day you discover you're rooming with someone who doesn't believe in deodorant. Or maybe boot camp makes you so miserable you wonder how you'll last one more hour, but you can't disappoint your parents by calling it quits because everyone from your great-great-great-grandfather on served his country and you can't let them down.

Or the person you planned to backpack with all over Europe fell in love and left you stranded at a youth hostel in Frankfurt to fend for yourself.

Or the job you had such high hopes for, the one you sailed off to in your new suit with your shiny briefcase full of dreams, turns out to be fall-asleep-at-your-desk boring or its own special purgatory, with a boss who makes your eye twitch, your face break out, and your hands tremble.

Maybe everything seems so clear and the road you travel looks freshly paved and clearly mapped. But one day you hit a pothole, then a detour, and find yourself lost. The road will split and you'll have to choose, and what if you choose wrong? Or the road will end and you'll be tempted to turn back. That's when you have to blaze a new trail.

You have to listen to the sound of your own soul. Deep down inside, you know what you are here for, what you are to be, what you are to do. It is where you will hear the deepest, clearest truth, away from the clutter and static and noise of the world. It is the place where you will hear God speak to you, if you are willing to listen. The journey to your soul is the only journey that matters. And to travel there, you must go alone.

You can scan college courses to figure out what to do with your life, question your friends to figure out what they are going to do, ask your parents and teachers for advice, fill out endless job applications, or check out the Army, Navy, Air Force, and Marine Corps.

But where is God calling you?

God has ordained a special place for you in this world that no one else can claim. It's up to you to find out where that is. You aren't ordered there, you're invited. To RSVP, you journey into your own soul and set aside what your parents want you to be, what your teachers told you to be, what your friends have decided to be. You go without the desires of everyone else. You leave behind the world's expectations. You take no one else's dream.

You sit in the silence of you and listen. You'll hear what some call the small, still voice of God and others call intuition. Then you feed the passion that burns in you, whether it is a flickering spark that confuses you or a roaring flame that consumes you.

It won't always be easy. You may be tempted to settle for less. You may worry about the competition. But no one else will be called to that one place that God has designed for you alone. No one can bring to that place your life experiences, talents, strengths, weaknesses, desires, and dreams. Your place in life doesn't belong to anyone else.

If you aspire to be someone else, you will fail. The world already has them. The world needs you.

The path you forge may not make sense to anyone else in the world but you. It doesn't need to. It belongs to you alone.

Start walking.

Harness the power of hope.

Every spring my friend Kevin calls to ask what message I'll share in my newspaper column for Easter.

I ask him what sermon he'll give, since he's a Catholic priest. We bounce ideas around, wander off into other topics, and then get off the phone without resolving the central question. We usually discover later that we ended up giving the same message.

One year Kevin asked me, "What gives you hope?" I didn't have an answer. Or maybe I had too many answers to settle upon one.

What gives me hope?

The first crocus that cracks through the earth. The budding lilacs. The smell of hyacinths. A bird's nest full of tiny blue eggs. The first butterfly sighting. Double rainbows.

Pregnant women and giggling brides. Watching a newborn

baby's fingers unfold in slow motion. Slivers of orange gold-fish swimming beneath the ice of a frozen pond.

Poems by Billy Collins, Adrienne Rich, and Gerard Manley Hopkins. Church hymns like "Amazing Grace," "Be Not Afraid," "How Great Thou Art."

A dandelion that pokes through concrete to find the sun. The last leaf in autumn that refuses to fall. Four-leaf clovers.

Van Gogh blue skies and Degas dancers in feathery skirts.

New sheet music. Voting ballots. The kindness of strangers.

Monks all over the world who pray daily for peace. Scripture readings: "Let not your heart be troubled," from John 14:1, and the promises in Isaiah 25:8: "He will swallow up death in victory; and the Lord God will wipe away tears from off all faces."

Each dawn that breaks through the darkness.

The life lessons of Max Cleland, Stephen Hawking, Rosa Parks, Anne Frank, Helen Keller, Beethoven, and Mr. Rogers.

The movie *The Shawshank Redemption*.

Pennies in fountains. Birthday wishes. First Communion dresses. A grand slam on opening day.

Newborn colts. A bakery full of wedding cakes. That random daffodil growing in the middle of nowhere. Students majoring in journalism.

Organ donors like my cousin's daughter, who gave sight to two people, and the one who gave my friend Beth the kidney that saved her life.

The nun who said, "I tried so hard to be good. But God doesn't need my goodness. He wanted my love."

One recovering alcoholic telling another one, "I think you have God traipsing all over you."

A plane taking off. Birthday candles, right before a wish extinguishes them. All the bridal parties posing by the fountains for wedding pictures at the Cleveland Museum of Art.

A blank page in a new journal.

The word *dayenu* repeated over and over during Passover to acknowledge "it would have been enough" to merely have been freed from slavery. To cross the sea. To find dry land. To eat in the wilderness.

My friend Debbie, who is deaf and understands me by reading lips even when I talk too fast.

Church marquees that carry messages such as "Is prayer your steering wheel or your emergency brake?"

A mud puddle full of splashing sparrows. The kind of sunset that erases away a bad day.

The words from *Cry, the Beloved Country* by Alan Paton, who described love as the only thing with complete power.

New voters. A child carrying a stack of books home from the library. Driving by a farm that still has cows grazing.

Psalm 43:3–4: "O send out Thy light and Thy truth: let them lead me; let them bring me unto Thy holy hill, and to Thy tabernacles. Then will I go unto the altar of God, unto God my exceeding joy."

The martyrs' chapel at the Jesuit Retreat House in Parma.

My nephew home from college who told me no, he didn't get taller since I saw him last, he simply stopped slouching.

The way a baby's head smells better than rain.

Country music songs that profess, "Love like you're not afraid of being alone." The Ursuline College writing student who told me, "A pen has no fear. A voice often does."

Psalm 30:11: "Thou hast turned for me my mourning into dancing: Thou hast put off my sackcloth, and girded me with gladness."

Authors Kathleen Norris, Joan Chittister, and Annie Dillard. Paul Schenly's piano students at the Cleveland Institute of Music.

Pussy willows.

The Carmelite nuns singing their hearts out on Easter morning.

The baby in the manger. The empty tomb.

Standing room only at Easter Mass. Purple crocuses bursting through the snow.

Farmers, artists, and poets. The light at dawn and twilight. Seeing the sun hit the grass and knowing that God has His eye on me.

The stories told by stained-glass windows.

A child holding a handful of fresh-picked dandelions like it's a bouquet of roses.

A perfect stranger saying "God bless you" when you sneeze.

A preschooler asking "Why?" for the hundredth time in five minutes.

A nursing home resident who can't remember her family but can recite every word of the Lord's Prayer.

Firefighters and police officers who place their lives on the line for complete strangers.

A teenager with purple hair and body piercings holding the door open for a woman with a double stroller.

Cancer survivors with new hair. Foster parents.

A one-year-old learning to walk. A stroke patient relearning to talk.

Nuns who still wear habits.

Birth announcements. Golden wedding anniversaries.

People who are willing to share what gives them hope, like Cleveland teacher Meryl Johnson. Here's what she heard when she asked her inner-city eighth graders at Charles W. Eliot Middle School what gives them hope:

When my grandma was sick in the hospital for three days and came home with a smile on her face ready to play a game of poker.—Drielle

Strolling through my urban area seeing that my neighborhood is gang free.—Curtis

Waking up in the morning with the scent of Dove soap on my face.—Mike

Playing on the basketball court and handling the ball with confidence.—Robert

Hearing kids laugh as they run around the park.—Jarrold

The smell of McDonald's hamburgers and fries on the kitchen table because my mom decided not to cook.—Demetrius

Sitting in my room reading *Forged by Fire*.—Timothy

My dad's strong arms wrapped around me when I need a shoulder to cry on.—Britnee

Seeing the bright moon shining in the corner of my window every night.—Lavelle

The smell of my grandmother's collard greens, macaroni and cheese, dressing, potato salad, ham, candied yams, and sweet potato pie on a Sunday.—Shameka

Hearing my father's deep voice.—Rashida

Putting my key in the door and walking into my beautiful home.—Jasmine

Having hot and cold water to use every day.—Katrina

Knowing if I leave it up to God everything will be okay.—Kiara

The high-pitched laugh of my newborn baby brother.—Brenton

The sweet smell of my house.—Antonio

Seeing my grandmom work in the fruit fields without her painkillers.—Chaz

Waking up in the morning and smelling my mother's cooking.—Paul

Not getting robbed again when I was walking home Saturday night.—Delonte

Praying to God, thanking Him for waking me up every day for the last 13 years.—Keyauna

The lovely poems and stories of Maya Angelou that let me be glad about who I am no matter what people say.—Nichole

I would add, "Having teachers like Meryl Johnson, who gives us all reason to hope."

What gives you hope? Scan your life and you'll find the answer everywhere.

Watch well your words.
Practice restraint of tongue and pen.

Before you say anything about someone, ask yourself three questions:

Is it kind?
Is it true?
Is it necessary?

The answer to all three would make for a quiet conversation for most people—myself included.

A while back there was a national public-service campaign to stamp out gossip with ads featuring Tom Cruise, Goldie Hawn, and Bette Midler.

In Ohio, a local rabbi created the "Words Can Heal" campaign to urge people to avoid *loshon hora*, a Hebrew phrase for "negative speech." The campaign spread across the country.

Rabbi Chaim Feld calls gossip the number one pastime in America. He wants to put an end to verbal violence.

The rabbi defines *loshon hora* as "any form of speech (gossip included) that might cause damage such as mental anguish, financial loss, physical pain, tarnished reputation, or the lowering of someone's esteem in others' eyes."

His efforts caught on fast. Bumper stickers came out with the words PUT THE BRAKES ON LOSHON HORA. One day I was sitting in a coffee shop when three people sat down nearby and started talking. When one woman began to criticize someone who wasn't present, the man across from her held up his hands to stop her and said, "We shouldn't be talking about her. She isn't here to defend herself."

The woman objected: "But it's true."

The man shook his head: "It still isn't right. This is *lona haran*, that Hebrew thing. We're not supposed to be doing this."

She continued, so the man shook his head and turned his chair away from her.

Recently a friend started to gossip, then stopped herself midsentence, "No, I'm trying to do that *losher hora* thing. Boy, it's really tough."

It's *loshon hora*, and I've been struggling with it my whole life. You don't know how much I've been dying to tell someone about a colleague who was spotted at a strip club. But I haven't. Yet.

Feld says that most people gossip to bond, to show off their wit, to cover for their lack of conversational skills, to get revenge, or to impress others. If his campaign is successful, gossiping might become as socially unacceptable as smoking.

But expect resistance. Some people get offended when you tell them you don't want to hear gossip. They think it's okay to share it as long as it's true or amusing.

The rabbi wants us to raise our standards. His book *Words Can Heal* offers these tips:

When it comes to offensive jokes, don't repeat them, and try not to laugh at them. When you get the urge to gossip, bite your tongue, change the subject, or walk away. When you're joking around, ask yourself at whose expense it is. When someone asks, "Did you hear about so-and-so?" answer something like, "No, and it's probably better that I don't." Don't repeat anything you wouldn't sign your name to.

And if those don't stop you, this Spanish proverb should: "Whoever gossips to you will gossip about you." That's a scary thought.

You never realize what a gossip you are until you try to stop. At first, you catch yourself every time you make a critical remark about people you actually like. Then, you stop yourself from spreading gossip about people you don't like. Finally, you find yourself getting uncomfortable as soon as someone else starts to gossip about anyone.

It's like quitting smoking. People who used to enjoy a pack a day kick the habit, then get irritated every time they catch a whiff of someone else's cigarette.

Gossiping is a tough habit to break. Putting someone else down lifts you up—for about five seconds.

Try stopping. I put myself on a no-gossip diet. If you think trying to quit smoking is tough, try to stop gossiping. You don't realize how addicted you are until you try to abstain. It's harder to lose five negative thoughts than to lose five pounds.

By the end of week one, I had failed miserably. I just had to tell a friend what I thought of the way one woman was parenting her children. I couldn't help remarking on how a woman in a bright giant multicolored sweater resembled a piñata.

If only Feld could create a patch we could wear that would deliver positive thoughts through the bloodstream directly to our brains. I've pondered wearing a rubber band around my wrist to zap myself every time I catch myself mentioning how goofy some guy looked combing a dental-floss strand of hair over his bald head. Forget the rubber band. My hand would fall off in no time.

Maybe I'm just a born critic. In a big family, you learn survival of the wittiest. You have to develop a knack for the put-down to survive older sibs who constantly tease that you're really not related to them and to fend off the younger ones who would follow you everywhere if you weren't mean to them.

My dad did his best to discourage unkind words. The only phone in our house—and we had 11 children—sat right smack on his desk in the dining room. Every time he'd overhear me putting down someone more popular than I was (which could mean anyone at high school), he'd scold, "That's not very nice," loud enough for the person on the other end of the line to hear. Or worse, he'd say, "Would you say that about her if she was standing here?"

Mom wasn't any help. She would admonish, "If you can't say anything nice about someone, don't say anything at all." Geez, Mom, if we all adhered to that philosophy, we'd all be silent as monks.

I'm not alone. Admit it. Don't you kind of enjoy gossip? It's one of life's guilty pleasures.

In my defense, I'm not as bad as some people who preface every comment with, "I don't know if it's true, but..." At least I have standards. The gossip has to be true before I pass it on. I've got a reputation to uphold. Who wants to listen to gossip that's wrong?

That was my lowly standard until the good rabbi gave me food for thought, the kind that's good for you, like brussels sprouts, but not particularly tasty. He has made me ask myself those three questions before I open my yap. Most of what I say doesn't pass the second question.

I'm not sure I can abstain forever, but I have cut down. By week two of my mental diet, I was thinking critical thoughts but had developed an EDIT button. Instead of every thought spilling out of my mouth like a gum ball, there was a momentary pause when my conscience showed up and said, *Don't go there.*

By week three, positive thoughts filled my brain. Only two out of every five negative thoughts made it to my mouth.

The diet hasn't been perfect, but I do feel lighter.

No matter what happens, don't take it personally. Take it spiritually.

My friend Veronica called one day and told me she was going to fax me an article that listed 27 ways to live a spiritual life. While waiting for the fax, I thought of what might be on the list. Probably some of the old standards like saying the rosary, reading the Bible, praying, going to temple, giving money to charity, meeting regularly with a spiritual guide.

Or maybe it would go a little further down the mystical path and suggest waking at dawn to pray the psalms, reading something profound by Thomas Merton or Martin Buber or Rumi, listening to Gregorian chants, or making a 30-day retreat.

When the list arrived, I had to check the cover letter twice to make sure I got the right fax. None of my ideas were listed in the article titled "27 Ways to Live a Spiritual Life Every Day" that appeared in the *Utne Reader*. The list originated in a publication called *Values & Visions* and consisted of excerpts from various books.

It offered the most basic things, like waking up. Isn't that a given? Ah, but there's getting up and waking up. Getting up is when you wake with a grumble and complain, "Good God, it's morning." Waking up is greeting the day with a cheer: "Good morning, God." I'll remember that when I'm tempted to hit the SNOOZE button for the third time.

Another tip was to play with a pooch. Dogs are Zen masters. They know when to eat, sleep, chase, and chill. Another idea was answering the door. Sounds simple, but how many of us avoid doing that when it's a stranger requesting a signature on a petition, a donation for the band boosters, or a pamphlet guiding you to their path to God. Welcome the stranger who rings the bell as if they indeed were a guest. A monk once told me if you are praying and you hear a knock at the door, go to the door, and make that your prayer. That sounds good in theory, but when I'm praying and someone knocks at my bedroom door to interrupt, it's hard to hear God in that knock.

Another tip was to take out the garbage. You can see even garbage in a spiritual light. The scent of a new rose and the stink of old broccoli offer flip sides of life. What we loved alive dies and becomes the garbage that then feeds something else to come alive.

Every experience, no matter how mundane or small, contains a lesson, a gift, a blessing if we take it spiritually, not personally. It doesn't matter if it's a job loss, divorce, speeding ticket, or health scare. Ask yourself, *What's the lesson here?* Learn it, practice it, be grateful for it, and move on. I once heard a man in recovery talk about how he ended up homeless and living at a shelter. There, he listened to an older man complain about how he had money but came to the shelter because his wife, his kids, and his boss were all driving him crazy. "The things you don't want to be bothered with are the things I'm looking forward to," the homeless man told the guy.

You can even take annoyances spiritually. One day I had my favorite blouse draped over my arm while I was shopping at Macy's. The air-conditioning in stores is so cold I brought the blouse in case it got too chilly. I shopped for a new comforter and sheets for our bed and took them to the car so I didn't have to carry them while shopping. At the car, a little voice inside urged me to leave my blouse in the car. I didn't listen. I went back and shopped for an hour. When it was time to leave, I realized the blouse had slipped off my arm. I had lost my favorite shirt in a clothing store. There was no way to find it. I pouted for an hour until I asked myself, *What's the lesson here?* A powerful one: Listen to your intuition or you'll lose your shirt. Losing my blouse might have kept me from losing something much more important.

Too often we try to find God by escaping our normal, ordinary, everyday life by doing what we think is spiritual—attending church, temple, or mosque; praying and meditating; reading the Torah, the Bible, the Koran, or the Bhagavad Gita.

What if we truly saw the spiritual in every challenge and challenging person?

What a life that would be.

My friend Ro lived that kind of life. She always took the aerial view. She had an uncanny way of scanning the view and finding God hidden in the scenery. She could always find the God in whatever was happening by finding the good in it. Some people wear their heart on their sleeve; Ro Eugene wore hers on her car. She drove around with a license plate that read: LUVUALL.

And she did. Ro loved everyone, even the people she didn't always like.

Those who knew her talked about the time her two oldest children came home from school one day after two kids around the corner had beaten them up. Ro took off like a bullet.

The rest of us would have yelled at the kids or their parents or called the police. Not Ro. She instantly put the second half of the Serenity Prayer to work and summoned the courage to change the things she could. She gathered up her husband and children and visited the home of the kids involved. The families ended up shaking hands and singing songs and forging peace that spread through the community.

Ro believed we're all spiritual beings having human experiences, that we're on earth to learn how to love, to take life spiritually, not personally.

We lost her the year she turned 79. When she completed her assignment here, I read in the obituary that Roslyn Eugene had founded a local Montessori school and taught school until she was 70.

She never stopped teaching. Ro believed that we all carry a spark of the divine. She was like the grand finale of fireworks. She was a spiritual superhero. She walked through walls. One time Ro was walking through her kitchen in the dark and slammed her shin on the dishwasher door that she'd left ajar. Instead of swearing, she praised God that she hadn't hit it harder.

When cancer hit, she gave it her all. When the chemo took

her hair, she wore an elastic ribbon with a bow around her bald head, the kind parents wrap around a bald newborn to prove it's a girl.

Ro only grew younger as she aged. We feared cancer would end the Curious Life of Ro Eugene, but it didn't. She was getting better the day her heart stopped. It shouldn't have shocked us that Ro wore her heart out, but it did.

A banner hung from the rafter at St. Cecilia Catholic Church proclaiming LuvUAll. After we set out food for the memorial, a handful of us prayed in a circle before the crowd showed up.

One woman said Ro taught her, "Hard is okay. You can do hard." Another offered, "It was never, 'You will be okay.' It was always, 'You are okay.'" I shared my favorite Ro-ism: "It's not impossible. It's just life."

I heard a new one: "If it was supposed to be different, it would be." Then we laughed. How do you cry for a woman who taught you, "Everything is okay. In this second, everything is perfect"?

It was. And it is.

The world needs your Yes!

I am being haunted by a paperweight.

Not just any paperweight.

This one spoke to me in the checkout line at a gift shop in Ann Arbor, Michigan. I wasn't sure if the paperweight was for sale or merely placed there as a message for shoppers, like a Thought for the Day brought to you by the store management.

The engraved rectangular slab of pewter taunted: *What would you attempt to do if you knew you could not fail?*

I tried to ignore it, but the small silver block parked near the checkout whispered to me, "What would you attempt to do if you knew you could not fail?" Okay, so the words were actually engraved on it, but I swear they spoke to me. I looked away. The paperweight tugged at my arm. I turned my back. It shouted at me.

I picked up the paperweight and held it in my hand for its answer as if it were a Magic 8 Ball, but heard nothing. When I looked at the price, I put it back. It cost $29. Too much to spend on myself, and if I bought it for someone else, I'd be too tempted to keep it.

I didn't buy it, but it followed me home, like a song that sticks in your brain and won't let go.

What would you attempt to do if you knew you could not fail?

What would I do?

Write a book, a play, or some short stories from the pile of ideas I've brainstormed and filed away.

I'd sing in a musical or join a choir and not worry about singing off-key. I'd go country line dancing in a pair of screaming red cowboy boots if I could trust my feet not to bruise the person next to me.

I'd take piano lessons and play on a baby grand in front of a big audience. I'd sign up for a drawing class or learn to paint. Every year I buy watercolors and pads but never pick up the brush.

I haven't come up with the one giant thing that's screaming to get out of me, but everyone else I've asked has. When I posed the question to the women at my beauty salon, it only took seconds for them to answer.

The owner said she'd go to medical school. One hairdresser said she'd hit on every single guy. Another one said she'd get married and have kids. Her biggest fear is failing at parenting. A woman getting her hair cut said, "I'd start my own business." Another hairdresser offered, "I would take up dancing."

Go ahead, pose the question. You'll be surprised at the

answers you get. Some people brush it off and say they would ask for a raise, buy a lottery ticket, or propose to Jennifer Lopez or Brad Pitt. One man, a successful local radio personality, surprised me with his answer. "I'd be a concert pianist," he told me.

There was something magical about that paperweight, so I called the shop to see if they still had it. Turns out they've gone through many of them. Everyone has the same reaction. The assistant store manager said everyone stops to read the paperweight and leaves talking about dormant dreams they plan to awaken.

I asked a group of friends what they would do. Gathered around a dining room table one December, we wrote down our answers and tucked them in envelopes to open next year. We all planned to take one giant step or many baby steps toward our dreams.

One wanted to go on a mission to Africa and fall "in like." She wasn't ready to fall in love, but was inching toward it. Another wanted to ask for a promotion and check out the Peace Corps. One wanted a new job and started looking.

Nearly every year since, we gather every December as one year comes to a close and another year teeters on the cliff ready to fall open, and we ponder that question or some variation of it.

What would we do if we weren't so afraid?

We open the sealed envelopes and find how life surprised us. The first year, the letters were more like yearlong to-do lists for self-improvement that included learning another language, traveling to another country, and writing a novel, play, or poetry.

We listed small steps and major dreams. One woman wanted to get her doctorate. Others wanted new jobs, new boyfriends, or new adventures. The next year we went deeper. Women wrote that they wanted to have a child. Fall in love. Get healthy. Grow closer to God. Feel less stressed. Love more freely.

Putting your hopes and wishes in writing helps them come true. We've made it an annual tradition. It's easy. Gather a few friends or family. Pass out some blank note cards or paper. Close your eyes and dream big. Then write it down.

It's better than making New Year's resolutions. We go around and share what we wrote, or pass if it's too private.

We try to start with the end in sight and ask ourselves: *A year from now, when I open this letter, who do I want to be?* Not in terms of income, status, or pounds on a scale, but in terms of what really matters. You put your name and the date on the front, then pack it up with the ornaments, clip it to December's page of the new calendar, or tape it somewhere you will hear it whisper to you.

I put mine in a ceramic fairy container my friend Vicki gave me. It sits in the room where I meditate. I say a prayer over the cards and my girlfriends. It's always a surprise to find what I wrote a year later. Here's how I fared one year:

Love life unconditionally. (Okay, so I loved most of it.)
Forgive everyone, everything. (Most people.)
Surrender every day to God's will. (Most days.)
Let go of fears. (Most of them.)
Measure my success at the end of each day by answering
   this: Did you love today? (Made progress.)

Hike every week. (Nope. But my friend Mena said, "If
   you haven't done it in a year, maybe you don't really
   want to." Good point.)
Love my mom more. (Check.)
Let go of work defining me. (Check.)
Let go of guilt motivating me. (Check.)
Let go of judging others. (Oops.)

After reading that long list, I wrote one simple word on the
card for next year: *Believe.*

I believe I can already feel it working.

I can feel myself say yes to life.

If you want to walk around the world like a human exclamation point, start saying yes to life.

Too often it takes a tragedy or a test result or a eulogy
to jump-start us into living. You don't have to wait for New
Year's Eve to get a clean slate. You don't have to wait for the
pathology report to come back positive before you embrace
life to the fullest.

Too often we try to improve our lives by saying no, by giving something up for months at a time or forever. We promise
to quit smoking, swearing, drinking, or overeating.

Why not practice saying yes?

What would it mean to say yes? It would mean that you
welcome every day with open arms. And at the end of every
day, stand out under the stars or open a window and drink in
the night, or hover over your sleeping child or spouse and simply rest in the stillness around you. As you soak up the quiet,
listen to what God is asking of you, then say yes.

To leaving someone who hurts you.

To staying with someone who loves you.

To forgiving the person who hurt you the most.

To accepting yourself as is.

To creating the thing you are most afraid to create.

To being happy with the way things are.

To hoping the best is yet to come.

To taking life less seriously.

To all the wonder and mystery and uncertainty and joy this world has to offer.

Empower your power by joining forces.

If only I had...If only I could...If only someone else would...

It's easy to feel powerless over injustices, disasters, diseases, and calamities. Even the small stuff that hurts people can leave me feeling overwhelmed and stressed out with guilt that I'm not doing more to help others.

Sometimes it's hard to know where to start. I have to remind myself that I might not have the power to make a global difference, but I do have the power to make a world of difference in the small place where I live and work. I just need to tap into the power I do have. And if it's not enough, I can combine it with the power of others and amazing things happen.

One day a woman contacted me at the newspaper where I work and asked me to help her recruit 100 women to raise $10,000 in one hour for a local charity.

What? The idea left me stunned.

Johanna Frebes has three boys, 11, 15, and 18. She lives in Cleveland and works as a compliance officer at a bank. She doesn't have time to volunteer. She's not alone. More people than ever are feeling pulled in a hundred different ways by commitments at home and at work. They no longer have the time to volunteer like they used to. They don't have the time or space on the calendar to schedule in two hours a week to volunteer at church, school, or in the neighborhood.

"I always felt guilty I couldn't do more," she said. "I can do one hour."

With her group, that's all it takes. One hour. Here's how it works.

One hundred women gather for one hour. The group even sets an egg timer for 60 minutes so the meetings don't go over the time limit. Every woman brings her checkbook and the name of a charity she'd like to help. The names of the charities are collected in a basket and three are chosen at random. The three women who suggested those three charities each give a five-minute presentation on why that charity is worthiest. Then they take five minutes to answer any questions.

Members then cast ballots to decide which charity will get all the money. As soon as the charity is chosen, every woman writes out a $100 check for it. Even if you didn't vote for the charity, you respect the majority vote and donate. Even if you can't attend a quarterly meeting, you send your check with another member.

The woman who suggested the charity gets to take the $10,000 or more in checks directly to the charity. At the next meeting, she shares how the money was used and what impact was made.

It's the perfect way to give for those who are busy and can't find time to volunteer, want 100 percent of their money going to a local charity, and want to be part of a group of generous, thoughtful people making a difference.

What a great way to maximize impact and minimize hassles. No "the check is in the mail." No treasurer. No keeper of the cash. No operational budget. No planning meetings that last an eternity. No walks, races, auctions, dinners, or dances to attend. Just one 60-minute meeting four times a year.

Johanna and her friend Kassy Wyman launched a website for 100+ Women Who Care—Cleveland Metro at http://100womenwhocarecleveland.weebly.com/. Johanna read a newspaper article about other cities that had started 100+ Women groups. In Dayton, the group raised about $18,000 per meeting. The money renovated a computer lab for the Boys and Girls Club, helped a family of Rwandan refugees, sent World War II vets to Washington, D.C., to visit memorials, and paid for dental care so homeless men and women could smile again.

The 100+ Women Who Care giving circle was created by Karen Dunigan in Jackson, Michigan. The first meeting in 2006 raised $10,000 to buy 300 cribs for newborns.

Some members set aside a little cash every day to build the $100 contribution. Others get their whole family involved. Every day, someone puts one dollar in the bucket.

Our first meeting was exciting. We ran out of chairs as the crowd grew in the back room at Brothers Lounge, a strange place to have an all-women gathering. Right away, we felt like sisters. We each signed a commitment form and picked a charity we wanted to plug.

I met women who were there to plug the Animal Protective League, the local historical society, Adoption Network, the USO, and an organization that provides uniforms for Cleveland schoolkids. It was interesting to learn about all the charities that spoke to the hearts of the other women present. I chose The Gathering Place, which offers free services for anyone touched by cancer.

The organizers welcomed us briefly, and then we set the timer and went to work. The beauty is that you get in, you give, and you get out, all in the span of one hour.

We put our charity forms in a basket and three were pulled out: the YWCA's Nurturing Independence and Aspirations program, the First Tee of Cleveland, and the Domestic Violence Center.

One woman gave a plea for the YWCA program that helps girls who age out of foster care and have nowhere to go. Once the girls turn 18, they leave foster care with a big garbage bag full of the little that they own in this world. Many of them end up homeless within a year. The YWCA was building 22 apartments for them. If we chose this charity, the money would cover new sheets, cookware, and other lifestyle needs for each girl to start out.

The audience drilled her with questions about the specifics of the apartments, the girls, and the need. After her five-minute speech and five minutes of Q and A, the timer rang.

Another woman urged us to choose First Tee, which teaches inner-city children ages 7 to 18 to live core values taught by golfing: honesty, integrity, sportsmanship, respect, confidence, responsibility, perseverance, courtesy, and judgment. The money raised would help cover a myriad of needs, including after-school programs and college scholarships.

The last woman pleaded with us to give to a domestic violence program for adults 60 and over who are abused by their own children, spouses, and caretakers. "There's a belief that it's too late to get help," she said. The group's motto is "Making tomorrow better than your yesterdays."

Ding.

It was time to vote. We each wrote down one of the three charities on a blue paper and tossed it in the basket. Then we pulled out our checkbooks. How exciting it would be to be the winner and walk into the charity of your choice with a pile of checks totaling $10,000!

It was a tie. We weren't sure what to do. Some wanted to divide the money between the two charities, others wanted to flip a coin. While we were trying to decide what to do, a woman who had come to observe the meeting signed a commitment form and cast a vote. It broke the tie. The YWCA program won.

Actually, we all won.

We raised $10,000 in one hour. We each used our power, and by combining, we made it 100 times more powerful.

You are a child's most important teacher.

Too many people put too much pressure on schools and teachers and public education to be all things to all students. The whole education system has been turned upside down by testing and the great expectations we place on others. What about our own role in being a child's teacher?

When I heard that a poor inner-city child from Cleveland got accepted to Harvard, I wanted to find out how she did it. Most of the poor kids in this town don't even graduate from high school.

Kim's mom, Maria Santana, welcomed me into their home. She was a single mom living on food stamps and welfare who lived near drug dealers that she kept praying away. Her kitchen ceiling was held together by strips of tape. One night when she was kissing her children good night, her foot crashed through the rotting floorboards.

Maria showed me the shoe boxes full of flash cards she made and a stack of workbooks she created from scratch. She told me how she always considered herself Kim's teacher, not just her parent.

"This is how I started," Maria said in hesitant English as she lifted the homemade workbooks out of an old shoe box. The purple cover she made for her daughter's *My ABC Book* had faded to lilac. *The Time Book* still had the clocks she drew on folded notebook paper. *My Color Book* showed an apple that is *rojo*, a balloon that is *azul*. Maria, who is Puerto Rican, taught her children Spanish.

She made wall calendars for Kim and Emanuel to learn numbers and dates. She graded the homework she assigned when they were two, three, and four years old. The *Facts About Me* book that Kim signed at age four says, "I want to be a doctor when I grow up." A heart-shaped magnet on the refrigerator held the Harvard acceptance letter in place, right next to the Spanish prayers reminding the family, "The Lord Is Our Protector," as if Maria needed reminding.

"Praise God" is the comma in every conversation. If it weren't for her two children and her faith in God, Maria would consider herself poor. How did a single mom living on welfare and food stamps raise a Harvard-bound daughter? Kim had access to the same teachers, books, and classrooms as the kids who drop out. The difference? Maria made parenting her number one priority. Not dating. Not drugs. Not bling. Not TV. Not complaining about the schools. Not feeling sorry for herself.

Maria gave 100 percent to her children. She took them on weekly trips to the library, not the mall. They lugged home

20 books at a time. She would read to them, they would read to her, then she made them read to the librarian. Maria made learning fun. When they read *Green Eggs and Ham*, she dyed eggs green for them to eat. Emanuel read 115 books before he started kindergarten. When he was three, he could read the Bible—in Spanish. They got so excited about reading that if Kim got in trouble, her mom threatened to take away her books.

When her disabled husband couldn't work, Maria stayed home to care for him. After they divorced, Maria earned $4.25 an hour as a clerk at the thrift store sorting clothes until the dust from other people's outfits made her sick. She bought her children the best clothes from the thrift store. One summer Kim earned more money than her mom. When Kim wanted to give the money to her mom, Maria wouldn't take it. Maria saved every tax refund until she had $7,000 to put toward a house. Maria never went to college. She saved enough from meager jobs to pay off her $15,000 house. Even after the children got scholarships for college, they took jobs and insisted they help out.

"God doesn't believe in sitting down," Maria taught them. "You do your part; God does His."

After the divorce, she turned to God as her partner. Her house isn't in the best neighborhood. She calls it the ghetto. One year, someone broke in and stole their radio and camera. A drug dealer lived next door until Maria prayed him away. She taped inspirational sayings all over the walls of her tiny home: *A Dios sea la gloria.* To God be the glory. She trusted even when a thief broke through the front door and again when one came through the back window. She slept with Kim to protect her daughter. "I trust God all the way, all the time," Maria told me.

She prayed on her knees at bedtime for her children, that classes wouldn't be too hard and that they would make good friends. She sat at the kitchen table constantly writing them encouraging notes. The pink kitten pad was for notes to Kim; the blue one, for Emanuel. She coached them over the phone, urging them to study hard and to have fun.

Maria never looked at herself as a single parent. "God is the head of this house," she said. She installed the linoleum floor in the hallway. She decorated the living room walls with photos of Kim and Emanuel and taped a collage of photos over her bed to dream about their new lives at college. Kim ended up at Harvard; Emanuel ended up in the honors program at Ohio State University on a full scholarship.

She knows there's no such thing as a single parent. Guidance counselors at the high school helped Kim get the classes she needed. A woman from a nearby private school helped Kim get into its internship program. A Harvard alum who is fluent in Spanish made Maria comfortable with Kim going there. A school adviser helped find scholarships.

Kim knows it all started with her mom. "She would do anything for us," Kim told me. "We're her world, her entire universe."

After Kim visited Harvard, she told her guidance counselor, "I just know I can provide a wonderful life for my mom."

Her mom would tell you she already has a wonderful life.

Four years after I first met Maria, Kim graduated from Harvard University with a degree in psychology. Three days later, Emanuel graduated from Ohio State with a degree in computer engineering. Maria bought them special graduation gifts from the thrift store and tucked them in bags surrounded by tissue paper. The two invitations to their graduation ceremonies leaned against the microwave where she could see them every day.

Ohio State University.

Harvard University.

She held the invitations to her chest.

"My heart is loaded with happiness. I love my kids."

That's where it all starts.

What you think about, you bring about.

I love the bumper sticker that reads: Don't Believe Every-thing You Think.

Oh, the nonsense my brain can conjure up. The fears. The resentments. The dramas. It's like a movie theater that plays the worst B movies some days.

My friend Aaron, who is a recovering alcoholic, said something profound once: "My brain is trying to kill me." I laughed, but realized it was true for me, too.

Imagine if you could record all those thoughts and play them back. I wouldn't stay friends with someone who was that negative and critical of me. Or as another friend in recovery said, "I need to evict those people who live rent-free in my head." Once you evict those thoughts, you can invite new ones in.

Wouldn't it be amazing to actually see your own thoughts

from a distance? I love that device in the Harry Potter books where you can download what's in your brain and see the cloudy haze of thoughts and memories that clutter your mind. It's called a pensieve and looks like a large, shallow, stone bowl. The fictional device allows one to extract their memories or excess thoughts and review them later on from third-person view and actually see the various patterns, links, and habits of thought that clutter the mind or that free it.

Usually the thoughts that bombard me are various forms of self-doubt. Who doesn't feel like a loser on the inside? Apparently a lot of us do. I once read a *Wall Street Journal* article that talked about the caustic commentary that runs through our heads. The headline grabbed me: "Silencing the Voice That Says You're a Fraud."

It turns out a lot of us play host to a parasite, an inner critic, a poorly behaved roommate. Even people who seem so successful on the outside, doctors, executives, and scholars, can have a constant companion in their heads that does battle and tells them they aren't good enough.

Do women suffer more than men? The verdict is out. I'm guilty of overthinking and so are most women I know. Most men I know seem to have an OFF button. They can hear bad news right before bed, worry for two minutes, say good night, and snore away. Meanwhile, their wives stay up half the night ruminating over the bad news.

Guys seem to go into their man cave to escape the noise. Maybe they don't have any noise in their heads and sneak away to escape what spills out of our noisy brains. I rarely know what men are thinking. When I ask my husband or sons, they usually say, "Nothing."

That's not true for all men. I've met a few men who suffer mercilessly. My friend Rob goes for a daily walk with his doubts and beats himself up for all his perceived imperfections and mistakes. He calls it his "daily flog."

Like Rob's, my brain manufactures all kinds of nonsense. I'm missing an OFF button, but at least I'm learning to turn down the volume on self-criticism. I had to after I scored off the charts on a *Wall Street Journal* quiz to see how self-critical you are. On the Dysfunctional Attitude Scale, I scored in the "high level of self-criticism and perfectionism" category.

I constantly believe people will think less of me if I make a mistake, when chances are good they aren't even thinking about me. Then again, because I am a newspaper columnist, some readers leave rants on my voice mail and nasty blog comments if they disagree with me, so it isn't always easy to set aside the negative.

I've tried replacing the negative with the positive. I taped affirmations inside the medicine cabinet and read them in the morning. What really changed it for good was when I realized that my thoughts have the power to create my life. What kind of life do you want to create? A scary one? A friendly one? A joyful one? A sad one?

I often pause to ask myself, *Do you want to be happy?* Then I tell myself, *Then let's think and act like it.*

So how do you evict the inner critic?

The counselors I've seen over the years, the books I've read, and my friends in recovery programs offer endless tips that have helped:

Keep a journal and log your thoughts. Go back and skim your writing weeks later to see what patterns hold you back.

Then decide how to break the pattern with new thoughts and actions.

Practice releasing negative thoughts as soon as they come in and you recognize them as unhealthy. I found it helpful to carry an extra positive thought written down on an index card in my pocket to use as a "thought replacer." It's something to read and say to myself again and again whenever doubtful thoughts seem to take over. Thought in, thought out, thought replaced.

Focus your attention on how you can be of service to others. When in doubt, help someone else and get out of yourself.

Distract yourself from overthinking. Every time you catch yourself stuck in worry, say something that lightens you up and distracts you from the worry. Use a word that jolts you away from the negative, like *banana split, sunflowers, vacation.*

Allocate half an hour a day to overthinking. Set aside one specific time to do it and remind yourself the rest of the day, *It's not that time right now,* and put those thoughts aside.

At the end of every week, jot down small achievements, victories, and blessings to savor.

It has also helped to use the advice of my friends in recovery. They constantly tell me to audit my thoughts, to not believe everything I think, but to question my thoughts and see if they're based on fact or fiction. I've learned to pause and ask myself: *Is this thought a fact or is it a fiction I've conjured up that scares me?*

Is there solid proof to back this up as a fact?

Does holding on to this thought enhance my life or diminish it?

Does thinking this way increase or decrease my chances of being more happy, joyous, and free?

Does thinking this way take me closer to the joy I want in my life or further away?

Pop. Pop. Pop. Pop. Those questions burst every thought bubble that comes to me. Laugh all you want, but give it a try.

I'm still working on remnants of the chronic "I'm not enough" message. One summer on the beach I prayed to be free of it once and for all. I looked to the horizon and asked, "When will I ever believe that I'm enough? How will that ever heal?"

The answer came swift and loud enough to hear over the crashing waves: *By helping others believe they are enough.*

Bingo. Even my inner critic liked it.

Aim higher.

Bonnie St. John lost her right leg at five years old to a bone disorder.

She jokingly refers to herself as a one-legged African American girl from San Diego with no money and no snow who took up skiing.

As a black woman with one leg, she's faced more hurdles than most. She's survived child sexual abuse, family dysfunction, divorce, race and gender discrimination, and navigating the world on an artificial limb. I met Bonnie at a conference in Worcester, Massachusetts. I was the breakfast keynote speaker; she was the lunch keynote speaker.

She wore a skirt and as close to heels as she could get while wearing a titanium leg. I loved that she didn't try to disguise her artificial leg.

"You want to see a miracle?" she asked the crowd.

She walked across the stage.

The audience went wild with applause.

Bonnie often goes to hospitals to visit patients and give talks to people who are facing obstacles that seem insurmountable like hers once did. She met one mother whose 13-year-old son had been horribly burned on his face and arms. The mother turned to Bonnie and asked, "Will my son ever live a normal life?"

I expected Bonnie to promise, "Of course he will." She shocked me with her answer.

"No," Bonnie said. "He should aim higher."

That's what she did.

Once she stopped trying to cover up her leg, once she stopped wishing she could be like everyone else, once she realized normal is highly overrated, she dared to dream bigger than a normal life and achieved it.

The little girl who had her leg amputated ended up being the first African American to win Olympic medals in ski racing. She won the silver and two bronze medals in downhill skiing at the 1984 Paralympics in Austria.

She aimed higher than being an athlete. She graduated with honors from Harvard University. She won a Rhodes Scholarship to Oxford. She was appointed to the White House National Economic Council under President Bill Clinton.

Her goal is to spread joy. She encourages people to relish the joy they already have. She doesn't just have a to-do list. She has a to-feel list and puts joy on it.

She's an author, executive coach, and inspirational speaker who had a quote end up on a Starbucks cup all over the country: "I was ahead in the slalom. But in the second run, everyone fell on a dangerous spot. I was beaten by a woman who got up faster than I did. I learned that people fall down, winners get up, and gold medal winners just get up faster."

What a great way to look at life. Everyone falls. The winners are the ones who get up faster and keep moving.

So many of us, myself included, want life to get back to normal when we fall down, when life pulls the rug out from under us. When I was diagnosed with breast cancer at 41, I kept waiting for my life to get back to normal. I thought it would after surgery, after chemotherapy, after radiation. It never did. I got a new normal. A better one.

Cancer treatments forced me to slow down my life. To reorder my priorities. To say no to what wasn't life. To say yes to what was.

Cancer forced me to aim higher. The scars from my double mastectomy serve as my daily reminder to say yes to life. Yes to writing the books I always wanted to write, yes to spending time with the people I love most, yes to embracing the joy in every moment of every day.

People all around us are living better-than-normal lives.

Years ago I interviewed a man who lost his hand in a work accident. When a guy like Ralph Colon loses a hand, he loses so much more than five fingers. Ralph had worked at Cardinal Fasteners and Specialties in a suburb outside of Cleveland for 28 years. He was adjusting the forging machine where he made bolts, giant ones, the kind that weigh up to 89 pounds. Ralph had to make a quick adjustment. When he reached his hand in, someone accidentally stepped on a pedal that released a clutch. He yanked his arm out, but too late.

The machine crushed his left hand.

Blood spilled everywhere. A medical helicopter rushed him to the closest trauma center. All of his fingers were dead. Doctors tried to save his thumb but couldn't.

That first year?

"I had a terrible way to go," Ralph said.

The amputation struck at the heart of what it meant to be a man. For the longest time he felt like half a man. One thought kept taunting him: *What good am I anymore?*

He was never the type to see a therapist, never one to take even an aspirin. But if not for therapists and antidepressants, he'd be dead.

"I would have shot myself," he told me.

Ralph always worked with his hands. The brakes on his car, the electrical work in the house, the plumbing—he loved hard work. An attorney suggested he live on Social Security Disability. Others suggested he live off workers' compensation.

He decided he would have to aim higher to be whole. He started up his own trucking delivery business. He named it R.L.C. Star Services.

R for Ralph.

L for Luana, his wife, his rock.

C for Colon.

And Star because when he looks in Luana's eyes, "It's like there's a star that's wrapped around the blue." She held on to him during those times when he nearly slipped away from the grief of it all.

Today, Ralph wears a bionic hand. He can pick up a pop can, but sometimes the hand opens and closes against his will. He's grateful to be alive, but some days are still hard.

"I have my days," he said. "Some days now and then I feel worthless."

On those days, he sits next to his aquarium and watches his fish swim until the bad thoughts float away. For a while he was mad at God. Not anymore.

"I was always looking for a challenge. I guess the Lord gave me one." He laughed.

He can finally shoot pool again, ride his motorcycle, and drive a truck.

"It's too easy to give up. Too easy," he said. "You find a way to make things happen. It might take ten times. It just takes me longer to do what I want to do."

Ralph likes to tell people about the mountain he climbed and what the view looks like from the other side now that his business is a success. He offers this advice for others: "Stay strong. Don't be afraid to start doing things with what you've got."

Don't be afraid to aim higher.

41

Make someone else's dream come true.

It's never too late to change the course of someone's life.

Six decades ago, Leonard Czartoryski had his life all mapped out.

He planned to be a dentist.

He served three years in the Navy in World War II in the belly of a plane as a turret gunner, then came home and used the G.I. Bill to go to college. He enrolled at John Carroll University in the summer of 1946. His wife, Joanne, raised their four babies while he worked days and went to school at night.

When he applied to dental schools, he heard grief about his complicated last name. Czartoryski was too foreign. Who would want to go to a Polish dentist? The teasing bothered him but didn't stop him.

He bought a class ring for 1949. The shiny amber ring was inscribed with the words *John Carroll University*. He wore it proudly, even though it would be 1956 before he finished all the coursework.

He had turned in his last paper and had just one final exam to complete. The day of the test, a big snowstorm hit Cleveland. He couldn't drive through the snow. It was too deep, too windy. The instructor didn't believe his excuse, made fun of his Polish ancestry, and insisted that Leonard would have to take the whole course over.

Leonard couldn't bear it.

He wasn't one to question authority. It was 1956, a time when children of immigrants accepted their lot in life. Discouraged, he quit.

Leonard took off his college ring. He even changed his name from Czartoryski to Cartor to shield his children from any prejudice they might face from such a heavy ethnic name.

For the next three decades, he worked at Lincoln Electric. He raised three boys and a girl who grew up hearing the story of how Dad almost finished college. Leonard retired in 1985, and then moved to Port Charlotte, Florida. At 85, he still felt the pain of that dream denied.

Then one day his son Tom told the story of the missed degree to a friend, Margaret Lahner. It bothered her so much that she wrote to Robert Niehoff, the president of John Carroll, and asked the school to award Mr. Cartor an honorary degree. Tom didn't tell his dad. He didn't want to get his hopes up.

It turned out that Leonard didn't have enough credits for the premed degree he had set out to get, but Beth Martin, associate dean of the college of arts and science, matched his old transcript with catalogs from 1949 to 1956 and discovered that Leonard had earned enough credits to graduate with a degree in sociology.

Tom called his mom. He didn't want to tell his dad over the phone. He feared the shock could cause another heart attack.

When he told his mom, "John Carroll wants to give Dad his diploma," she burst into tears. When Leonard heard the news, he couldn't speak. He went into his bedroom and opened the jewelry box. He dug through a pile of cuff links and pins for his 10 years, 20 years, and 30 years of service at Lincoln Electric. There it was.

The amber class ring still shone.

It no longer fit his ring finger. All those years of winding coils through his hands had left his fingers calloused and swollen. Leonard slid the ring onto his smallest finger.

When the graduates lined up that spring, all 990 of them, Leonard wasn't among them. He was on oxygen and too frail to travel. But up onstage, sitting in the VIP section, his son Rick came forward when they called this name: Leonard N. Cartor.

The degree he earned more than 50 years ago was finally his.

He was a college graduate at the age of 85.

The John Carroll graduates weren't the only ones to hear his name read. Another crowd of graduates heard his whole story.

Denise San Antonio Zeman, president and chief executive of Saint Luke's Foundation, read the newspaper column I wrote about Leonard's dream come true. She decided to change her graduation speech for the Case Western Reserve School of Dental Medicine. She told the Class of 2009 receiving

Doctor of Dental Science degrees about Leonard Czartoryski, who 63 years earlier had dreamed of becoming a dentist.

Denise summed up the journey Leonard took, from his World War II service to his night classes at John Carroll to the snowstorm and mistreatment over his name. She told the graduates about how he worked hard, raised a family, but never fulfilled his dream.

Leonard's family cried later when they heard that each graduate standing at the edge of their dream to be a dentist had learned of their father. Denise told the graduates:

Today, as you receive your degrees as dentists, Leonard's son is standing in for his father, now too frail to travel, to accept his diploma with a degree from John Carroll University, and Leonard, whose ring finger is too calloused and swollen to bear the class ring, now wears it proudly on his smallest finger.

I ask you, the Class of 2009, you who have fulfilled your dream of becoming dentists, to pause for a moment and think about the story of Leonard Czartoryski, a story of a man who dreamed of standing where you stand today, but a man whose seasons of life have taken him in different directions but whose dream of earning a college diploma will become a reality today.

Denise told the graduates that everyone they met in the past four years came along for a reason, a season, or a lifetime:

Perhaps some of the people you've encountered along this journey were there to teach you an important lesson.

Or maybe you have been in someone's life for a reason. A clinic patient whose pain you relieved, a child who was inspired by the fact that you gave him his first toothbrush.

My hope is that when someone down the road asks you to help someone in need, you will remember that perhaps this is your chance to be in someone's life for a reason.

Leonard Cartor missed out on becoming a dentist, but he got to change the ending to his life story. And he got to influence the beginning of those graduating students' life stories, for a reason, for a season, and perhaps, for a lifetime.

Triage.

The ambulance competition started when each rescue squad was handed a typed sheet of paper stating the problem we were all about to encounter:

Your unit is called to the scene of an auto accident at 3:30 p.m. on a Saturday. The temperature is 35 degrees and what had been snow has turned to rain. As you arrive at the scene, you see that one auto has slid into a post causing the fuel tank to rupture, spilling a large amount of gasoline over the area. The engine is running wild. A large crowd is gathering as you go to the auto and find the following: The windshield on the passenger's side is cracked.

Victim number one, the driver of the auto, is slumped over the wheel. He has a deep laceration across the bridge of the nose extending down the right side of the nose into the cheek, bleeding moderately. The victim is semiconscious, and has a badly deformed right leg at the ankle at which point there is also severe bleeding. As you are working on the victim he seems to be trying to tell you something.

Victim number two, the passenger of the auto, is unconscious and leaning against the right-hand door of the auto. The victim has an incised wound about five inches long across the forehead at the hair line, which is bleeding freely. Both wrists seem deformed.

Go!

Our team scrambled into action to treat the fake victims on the gymnasium floor. We quickly triaged the situation and decided what was most urgent. Control the bleeding on both victims with direct pressure. Turn off the car engine, warn the crowd not to smoke, call the police and fire departments. Check for other injuries. Check for medical ID alerts. Treat both victims for shock. Suspect head, neck, and back injuries on both victims and immobilize them for transport. Splint the wrists on victim two.

We ended up winning that statewide ambulance competition back in 1977, back when I was an emergency medical technician for the Kent State University Volunteer Ambulance Service. We competed in the first-aid competition with EMTs from all over the state. I also worked at a funeral home that offered ambulance service for my hometown back then, when the funeral homes in small towns ran the ambulance services, not fire departments.

Besides lifesaving first aid, the training to get certified as an EMT taught me how to prioritize my life for the rest of my life. The instructors pounded into us one word: *triage.*

Triage is the way you determine the priority of treating patients based on how critical they are. Everyone can't be treated first, so triage is how you sort them by priority and choose what order to take care of everyone. It comes from the French word *trier,* which means to sort or select. In World War I, French doctors in the battlefields set up a system to decide how to divide up the wounded.

When you get to the scene of an accident, you don't treat the person who is screaming the loudest or bleeding the fastest or complaining the most. You scan the entire scene as fast as you can and treat the person who is the most critical. Does the person have a heartbeat? Is the victim breathing? Heart and airway concerns trump fractures and bleeding. You can apply the concept to your family when everyone is pulling on you at once for time and attention.

We were taught the ABC's: airway, breathing, circulation. Life-threatening injuries come first, then limb-saving injuries, then everything else. We practiced for mass casualties, where you have to quickly sort out whom you can save and whom you can't, who needs immediate care and transportation and who will have to wait.

At first you feel overwhelmed. Where do you start? You identify the people who need care first, those for whom immediate medical care and transportation could make the difference between life and death. You try not to get sidetracked by the enormity and drama of the situation. You put each victim into a category.

Urgent and immediate victims are the highest priority: They need immediate attention to save a life or limb. They need CPR or surgery and must be transported first. Their survival is at stake, so they have to be stabilized and moved fast.

High-priority victims are more stable but must be watched carefully and receive medical care and attention within hours or they could become an urgent priority.

Nonurgent victims need medical care but can wait if necessary to get it from a doctor and might not need the ER.

You can apply the concept of triage to other occupations as well. I was in a classroom once and watched a teacher assert crowd control by triage. "I only want to see a hand if you are bleeding or on fire. Everything else can wait," she told the students. A hand went up. "Are you bleeding or on fire?" the teacher asked. The hand went down.

I use the concept of triage to keep my life in balance. I pause to weigh any situation I'm drawn into and decide, based on the resources I have within and around me at that moment, what I can and cannot do. It's fluid and changing depending upon the day I'm in and the calamity or calm around and within me.

Every day I order my priorities. The motto "First Things First" guides me. It originated in that Scripture reading, "But seek ye first the kingdom of God, and His righteousness; and all these things shall be added unto you." It helps me to prioritize my day. Before jumping into work, I fall to my knees. Prayer and meditation are my lifeline. They give me the clarity I need to see throughout the day what is mine and isn't mine to do.

On a day when the world is pulling at me in a dozen different ways and I can't say yes to everyone, I pause to triage:

What is most vital? My relationship with God comes first. Then my health. Then my family. Then my closest friends. Then my work/mission in life. Then the greater community around me. If I'm not sure where to start, I begin at the top of the list, not the bottom. Some weeks are so busy that I never get to the last tier, but the most important relationships don't suffer.

I even made a big target on a sheet of poster board to help me stay focused on what to say yes to and what to say no to. In the center bull's-eye I wrote my name, God, and the people I love the most, my husband, kids, and grandchild. In the next circle, I put the names of my siblings, Mom, and closest friends. In the third circle, I wrote the names of the more distant friends and acquaintances. In the last circle were all those projects that never need to be done and concerns that I have no power or influence over in life. Most days I never make it to that outer circle, and that's okay, because I've taken care of the most important people and projects.

If you know your target and aim for the bull's-eye, you don't waste a lot of energy in the outer rings of the target that aren't urgent and important. Instead of using a shotgun to hit the target and scattering your energy everywhere, you use the rifle approach and aim for one clear focus in the center and hit it.

Looking at that target helps me to see that some priorities aren't mine to handle. I can't save every person or fight for every cause. In those outer rings of the target, I write in things that concern me that I have little power to change, like global warming, saving the whales, the politics of North Korea.

I give myself permission to release that which I cannot save, all those projects, plans, and people who aren't my responsibility. I pause, hold them all up in prayer, bless them, and release them.

And in doing so, I release me, to be my best self where I'm needed most.

A saint is someone who knows how much God loves them.

My mom has a special holy box in her bedroom. The wooden box hangs on the wall across from the foot of her bed. Behind the glass window it holds a dozen round containers the size of a quarter. Inside each, behind a layer of glass, are relics of the saints, bone chips no bigger than a speck.

Saints were big in our house. Huge. A four-foot-high statue of Mary standing on the cedar hope chest looked over my parents in their bedroom at night. How they conceived 11 children in that room is beyond me.

We grew up reading *The Lives of the Saints*, standard Catholic literature in every house. After a few chapters, you got the picture of what sainthood entailed, and it wasn't pretty. Saints were beheaded, burned alive, tortured, and raped. It seemed that only virgins and martyrs need apply for canonization. Sanctity required superhuman suffering and sacrifice.

We were all named after a saint three times: our first name, middle name, and confirmation name. You had to be named after a saint. At birth, your parents chose the name of a saint as a model and guardian over their child.

To choose our confirmation name, we flipped through volumes of the lives of the saints to find out how they were martyred. On Halloween at Immaculate Conception School, we were encouraged to dress up as saints. Most kids chose costumes to depict Saint Patrick with his staff driving out snakes, Saint Francis in a brown robe and a rope belt, Saint Nicholas in his Santa suit. A few kids tried to pull off Joan of Arc, but the nuns frowned upon wearing makeup to look like burns.

The Vatican enforced rules about who was a real saint. You needed proof in the form of miracles, at least three. There was a saint for every occasion, disease, and problem. Saint Christopher served as the patron saint of travelers. Chris was magnetically stuck to our dashboards until a pope came along and demoted him.

Saint Joseph is the patron saint of Realtors. If you can't sell your house, you bury Joe in the yard upside down and a SOLD sign magically appears out of the grass a few days later.

If you lost something, you prayed to Saint Anthony, who ran the cosmic Lost and Found. We'd pray, "Something's lost and must be found, please take a look around. Dear Saint Anthony, we pray, bring it back without delay." And voilá, the purse, the wallet, the $5 came back like a boomerang.

If you lost something more important, like your mind, you prayed to Saint Jude, the patron saint for hopeless causes.

Saints were our liaison to God. In the holy lineup, Mary was the marquee player, the queen of mercy and of love.

Nearly every Catholic has heard the story about how heaven was filling up with all sorts of undesirables. When Jesus complained to Saint Peter about letting them in, Peter said, "Don't blame me. I turn them away from the pearly gates and Your mother lets them all in the back door."

There's also the popular sermon about the boy who kept praying to Jesus for a bicycle but never got it. One day the kid wraps up a statue of Mary and hides it in the closet. Then he folds his little hands together and prays, "Jesus, if You ever want to see Your mother again..."

In time, I came to realize that holiness and halos weren't merely for those stained-glass saints. There are unofficial saints among us, people who simply love God and others without any blood and gore to show for it. People like my uncle Johnny.

He had X-ray vision. He could see God in everybody. I never knew that until I started reading his daily e-mails. For months he sent them with Gospel excerpts. At first I deleted them without a glance, then one day I scrolled down and read one of his personal reflections that followed the Scripture passage.

My dad's youngest brother never tried to be profound, never tried to convert, never tried using Christianity as a club. He saw the holy in the ordinary, in the average, in the unpleasant. He turned problems into parables, like the night his furnace quit:

I called Rick Swan who had helped me once before,
he wasn't home so I began taking the blower apart
afraid some forgotten step would end in a night without heat.

As I tried to remove the motor from the blower cage, the
*   phone rang.*
It was Rick, who talked me through the procedure.
It was as if God was standing nearby, reminding me of
*   my dependence on him.*

He saw God's reflection in his wife, Barbara, in the ten
children he raised, in every stranger he passed:

Like all the everyday faithful
I have known loneliness,
been stuck on freeways with stalled cars,
mopped up the vomit when children fought the flu, or some
*   unknown virus.*
Nevertheless, He has embraced me, has made His presence
*   known to me.*
Often in the person of Barbara, or sunshine on the marsh
*   filled with green;*
or when I sit silently
He interrupts the breaths that come and go
with a mysterious nudge suggesting that I whisper His
*   presence to a three-year-old*
or the cart boy at Marc's Deep Discount Store.

One day he e-mailed a list of sacred places. It included the
swimming hole he used as a boy. The tool repair room at the
Cadillac tank plant where he worked. University Hospital's
Ireland Cancer Center. Aisle one of Marc's Deep Discount
Store.

He turned a past of poverty into a litany of gratitude, recalling tender mercies granted to him by the midwife on the farm my grandpa lost during the Depression. By the first black family he had ever met, who came to his First Communion. By the boy who carried him on bike handlebars to basketball games.

He thanked strangers he never met, migrants who picked the bananas he ate, the Chinese woman who sewed the parka that kept him warm.

Uncle Johnny was a radical Christian, something rare in a culture that values justice over mercy and compassion.

> *Love your wife, your mother and father,*
> *your teacher, who bores you to death, your annoying brother,*
> *Like Mary and Joseph you present to Jesus*
> *everyone you meet,*
> *cashiers at the Giant Eagle, drivers who talk on cell phones,*
> *friends, memories of those you love—long dead.*
> *What a privilege to share in Jesus' Calvary, and bring*
> *His amazing grace to an unknown.*

Amazing grace. That's what he was full of, right until the end.

When he died at 77, they placed him in the strangest-looking coffin. It was so deep, you had to bend over it and peer in to see him. The coffin was homemade. When my uncle was going through treatments for cancer, he and my aunt discovered a little Amish boy who needed a ride to the hospital for leukemia treatments. My uncle and aunt brought him to and from the hospital. The boy's family made my uncle's coffin.

I miss my uncle's daily e-mails but still see his daily reflection in the cart boy at Marc's, in the drivers on their cell phones, in the everyday faithful. There are relics of saints everywhere, all around us.

I once heard it said that a saint is someone who knows how much God loves you. To know that fully means you live without demands on others for anything; it's a love of God and others carried to extravagance.

You don't have to possess supernatural powers to be a saint. It doesn't mean you are above being human. It means you are fully human. Sainthood isn't reserved for a chosen few, it's demanded of the many.

Don't quit before the miracle happens.

The family needed help.

Doctors had given up on their son. Put him in an institution, they said.

The family refused.

The Johns family moved to my hometown of Ravenna, Ohio, back in 1969, when I was in eighth grade. Someone in our church found out they needed help and decided to recruit students from the Catholic grade school to help. A woman in our church took a handful of us to volunteer at his home.

Diane Plough had a gentle soul and wanted to teach us to be of service to others. We already spent one Sunday morning a month volunteering at church making donuts from 6 a.m. to noon to sell as a fund-raiser. Wasn't that enough?

Diane wanted us to help Tommy. He was severely developmentally and physically disabled. Our job was to spend

Saturday mornings "patterning" him. The family needed a team of people to come by twice a day to exercise him. Diane brought the five of us.

I hated going at first. It was hard work and didn't seem to make any difference. At least not any you could see. But I liked Diane. She was pretty, with flaming red hair, and she treated us like we were young women, not kids in grade school.

Week after week, we spent hours in Tommy's basement trying to get him to crawl through a contraption on the floor. It was like a tunnel made of wood with string over the top in a crisscross pattern to keep him from escaping. We had to force him to crawl all the way through. He hated it. So did we. He'd moan and groan and claw at the string and get stuck and fight as we untangled him.

The basement looked like a physical therapy room with all kinds of areas set up to exercise and stretch Tommy. He had to be patterned morning and evening. It took five people, one to hold each limb and one to hold his head. He lay on a table and one of us was stationed at each arm and leg to move it on command. It was like making him swim in the air. One person held his head down and turned it side to side. No one wanted his head. He'd drool and spit and grab your hair. You had to be careful not to get your fingers near his mouth or he might bite you, at least that's what we were told. We heeded the warning.

We were 13 years old; Tommy was two years older. He seemed much younger as he yanked our hair and waved his arms and legs around and grunted. He couldn't do anything on his own, not even sit up, crawl, or feed himself. The whole ordeal of exercising him must have been painful for him, but we had to move his muscles so they wouldn't atrophy. He fought every movement.

Tommy was skinny, with dark short hair. He couldn't talk. He could only grunt, cry, laugh, and wail like an animal. He was strong, so it was hard to force his arms and legs to go in directions he didn't want to go. It was a workout for everyone. The only payoff came at the end of each session, when he knew we were done working on him and he'd relax and smile and laugh and seem overjoyed to see us.

In all that time, I didn't see any progress, not a smidge. We kept going every week because Diane saw a spirit in him that we couldn't.

What was the point, I wondered, but never out loud. Tommy would never get better. And he didn't. Not while I was volunteering. But the experience taught me to be of service, and I went on to volunteer elsewhere in high school. A few years after I stopped helping Tommy, I was volunteering at Happy Day School for the multiply handicapped. I was teaching kids who had to wear helmets how to make the sound of alphabet letters. I'll never forget the day I noticed a young man standing at the end of a hall. He looked familiar. It was Tommy.

He was not only standing.

He was walking.

I couldn't believe it. The miracle happened. I had given up, but the rest of the volunteers hadn't.

It turns out Tommy only walked for a year, and then his hips got dislocated and gave out. His parents didn't want him to have to go through surgeries that might not work. He ended up getting around in a wheelchair. He's in his fifties and lives in a group home. His mom, Jean, visits him every day. His dad passed away a few years ago.

Jean still doesn't know how much he understands, but says Tommy has a built-in timer. He knows when she's supposed to visit and gets upset if she's not there on time. He starts laughing when he sees her. She entertains him with musical toys that light up and make sounds. She loves that he hums when he's happy.

It wasn't until decades after coming to her home that I learned about her life. She told me that her first baby died three days after birth. Then Tommy came along. He suffered from lack of oxygen before, during, or after his birth. They didn't know for six months, when he wasn't showing signs of progress, that he was profoundly mentally and physically impaired. He couldn't sit up and didn't make noise. At first Jean was bitter. But her husband consoled her, telling her, "Tommy doesn't know he's different."

They prayed a lot. Then they lost another child, a son who died at nine years old from chicken pox. They ended up with one healthy son, David.

To Jean, the miracle of Tommy wasn't that he walked. It was that he got to socialize with all those people who came to help for all those years. Tommy got to be part of a rich, caring community. He wasn't isolated at home or tucked away in an institution. He had friends who came every day to see him. So did his family.

"I met so many nice people through him," Jean told me. "He's my little angel. He shaped my whole way of life."

He shaped my life, too. Tommy taught me to give of myself. I went on to volunteer at Happy Day School, at American Red

Cross blood drives and their disaster services, and at the Kent State University Volunteer Ambulance Service.

Tommy shaped Andrea's life, too. She saw something in him that I missed.

"There was something there," she told me. "I think there was more to him than what we thought."

When Tommy grabbed her hair to play, she'd think, *I know you're in there.*

Tommy helped shape her philosophy for life. "I'm not here for me," she said. "I'm here for others. We pull each other through."

Tommy taught us all that you can't ever give up.

You can't quit before the miracle happens, and there might just be more than one miracle.

*Make amends as soon as
you can, while you still can.*

Make the call. Send the card. Bury the grudge.

"Whatever it is you have, put it to rest," Larry Goodman Jr. told me as he prepared to put his dad to rest at the Starlight Baptist Church.

"Let that mess go," he said. "Let it go."

He and his dad stopped talking one August. He never imagined the silence would last eight months. The two broke off contact after they disagreed over Larry's wedding arrangements and his dad showed up late for the ceremony.

For the longest time, neither man would budge. Those eight months were tough on both men. Larry, 27, missed his best friend, the man who taught him how to pick friends and choose women, the man who taught him how to grill ribs and make the best lima beans north of Georgia, the man who taught him how to be so stubborn.

Then one day his father ended up in the hospital with chest pains. Larry stopped by and brought him a card. Larry hadn't planned on mending things, but the moment his dad saw him, his father smothered him in hugs. They got a second chance.

"When I got through the door he was hugging and kissing on me," Larry said. "I was trying to put the hard role up. I was still mad."

His dad made peace with his son with these words: "I know you're mad at me, but I love you and I know you love me, too. I'm always here for you."

Then they went back to being best friends.

"It just went back to the way it was," Larry said, tears filling his eyes. He had been crying ever since he got the call a few days earlier. He had been talking to his sister on the phone when someone clicked in to break the news. When his sister got back on the line, she screamed, "Our father's dead!"

There had been a house fire. Larry drove over to his dad's home. He didn't believe the news until he smelled the smoke. By the time he arrived, the charred house was already boarded up. Larry had to identify the 220-pound, six-foot-four bearded black man at the coroner's office. He knew it was his dad when he saw his father's legs. Larry has the same muscular calves.

Larry emptied out his dad's locker at Ford Motor Company where his dad had worked for nearly 29 years. Larry always figured his dad, who was only 48, would retire from there. As he dug through his father's work clothes, the tears fell.

"Every time I pulled an item out of his locker," he said, "I felt like a little boy waiting for my daddy to come around that corner."

That little boy used to have a clock inside him that knew

what time the train delivered his father, to a boy who would run nearly a mile to greet him. He thought of the time his dad took him to his first baseball game and how his dad could make anyone laugh and how his father gave up so much to work second shift.

"I wish that when I played basketball in high school I could have looked up in the stands and seen him sitting there," Larry said. "What I'll miss is when I told my father about something that happened to me—I don't care what it was—he'd take the negative out of it. Whatever small part that was positive that could come out of it, he'd say, 'How can you make that work for you?'"

Larry found that one small positive part when he spotted a bottle of cologne in the locker.

"My father loved the way that Jovan Sex Appeal for Men smelled," Larry said, laughing hard. "Oh, man, one time when I was at his house—I was about 20—he said, 'I got something really good.' He took me all the way upstairs, saying, 'You're going to like this.' And he pulls out that bottle of Jovan."

Larry wore one of his dad's suits to the funeral, plus a few dabs of that Jovan Sex Appeal.

Larry shared his story with me to encourage others to make amends while they can. I'll never forget the time I interviewed a man who waited too long.

William S. and his teen daughter, Becky, had once been close. When she was a toddler, she'd climb onto his lap and snuggle, safe and secure against his chest. After long days at the office, he'd come home, take off his tie, and leave the knot in place so Becky could grab both ends, pull, and make it disappear.

Father and daughter were best of friends, even after he and her mom split up. Then came the teen years, when loyalties stray, when friends matter more, when challenges to parental authority create a gulf between generations. They had a fight and stopped speaking. A year passed. He knew the gap wasn't insurmountable. It would just take time to bridge it. The day would come when he would take his daughter's hand and they would talk.

Then one Friday he came home to a blinking answering machine. Becky, who was 17, had been in a car accident. The Jeep Cherokee she was riding in swerved in the snow, flipped several times, and landed upside down. Becky had a broken pelvis, broken ribs, and a fractured skull.

By the time he arrived at the hospital, she was gone. He sat down next to the gurney that held her body. He wrapped his warm hand around her cold fingers and looked into her bruised face. She was only a senior in high school. For two hours, he wept and told Becky that she meant the world to him, that he loved her, that he wished he had been there all those missed months.

He prayed for a miracle, prayed that she would squeeze his hand, that she could talk with him, just for a few minutes. He told her everything he wished he had said while she was still alive.

I'll never forget him sharing that last moment with her. So many of us could end up with regrets like that. Almost every time I do a book signing, a mom or dad will come to the table and confide that they haven't spoken to a son or daughter in years. Everyone is waiting for the other person to budge.

Why not make the first move? My friends in 12-step

recovery programs have taught me that there shouldn't be any relationships left with bitterness or resentments surrounding them. They encouraged me to write down a list of all the people I have harmed, either by my action or by my inaction, and look solely at my part when it comes to repairing the relationship.

Then I take the list to God and pray for the willingness to make amends. I no longer wait for the other person to budge. I don't need to wait for them to take care of their part. That may never happen. I take care of my part, even if it's smaller. When I do, they almost always acknowledge their part, too. But even if they don't, my mind and heart are clean.

Sometimes I have to pray for the willingness to make amends, but it always comes, and thankfully, it hasn't come too late.

What's keeping you from making the first move?

*Silence the noise. In times of doubt
or indecision, pause and make
room for God.*

The noise usually starts up as soon as the wait begins.

It doesn't matter if I'm waiting on good news or bad news, whether I'm on the mountaintop or in the valley, all matter of doom-and-gloom scenarios appear. My first instinct is to interview everyone I know for an answer, which usually adds to the noise.

There have been two times in my life when I experienced the gift of silence in such a profound way that it felt holy.

The moment I found a lump in my breast back in 1998, the voices started up full force: "It's just a cyst...It's a benign lump...It's cancer." Everyone had a story that ended well or a horror story that ended tragically, about their mom, their aunt, their sister, their dog that died of cancer.

I tried to shut out all the noise and prayed for a plain, boring, thank-my-lucky-stars benign lump. Deep in my gut, I was terrified. The lump had grown so fast. As I waited for the lab results, the lump seemed to grow larger with each passing day. At first it seemed to be as big as an almond, then the size of a walnut half, then a whole one. Maybe *I* was just going nuts. I couldn't turn down the fear swirling around in my head.

Then late one night as I was driving home from giving a talk at a church retreat, I found myself lost on a dark winding road in the Cuyahoga Valley. It was almost midnight and I was an hour from home. The trees grew close to the road and the fog rolled in from the river, hiding the way out. I slowed to a crawl. Suddenly, deer appeared all around me. I was driving in the middle of a herd of deer. I had to go five miles an hour so I wouldn't hit any of them. They took their time, meandering around my car, leisurely strolling across the road.

Then a calm swept over me. The deepest peace emanated through me. I sat in complete silence. All the noise was gone. The quiet acted like a great eraser. It took away the confusion and the fear and the endless chatter in my brain. The drive became a prayer. Somehow I knew in that moment I would be okay, even if the lump was cancer. I've never forgotten the gift of those deer, the gift of that silent night, the gift of that peace.

It made me realize that sometimes being lost is part of the long journey called life. I wouldn't always choose the detours I end up on, like the Cancer Road, but those routes sometimes choose me and lead me exactly where I'm supposed to be.

The other time I experienced the gift of silence was when I was waiting for what I knew would be good news. My whole life, I wanted to be a writer. The day arrived when it was time to talk to a list of publishers who had seen my manuscript *God Never Blinks*. I flew to New York City to meet people at eight different publishers. Before I left, everyone and her brother tried to give me advice. Don't give away the foreign rights. Hold on to movie rights. Don't sign anything without an attorney reading it. Noise, noise, noise.

It was December and the city was crazy with Christmas shoppers and holiday events. I stayed at my sister's apartment on the Upper East Side and her husband took me on the subway and dropped me off on my agent's doorstep so I wouldn't get lost.

My agent, Linda Loewenthal, took me from publishing house to house. It was both exciting and terrifying. After we met with the first batch of publishers, the noise grew even louder. It was hard to silence all the what-ifs going through my head.

In between interviews, I went window-shopping to distract myself. My cell phone rang while I was in a store that afternoon.

"Get to my office," Linda said excitedly. "We have an offer. We have to give them an answer by 5 p.m. Call your people."

My people?

"I don't have any people," I told her.

"Your husband, your children," she reminded me.

Oh yeah, my family. Those are my peeps.

I hopped in a cab, called my family, told them what was going on, and tried to catch my breath. Once I got to Linda's office, she gave me all the details. I spent the next couple of hours mulling over the offer versus the strong interest we had from other publishers.

My head was spinning. I loved the team at Grand Central Publishing, and the offer was generous, but was it the right amount? Was this the home for the manuscript I'd sweated over and cherished as if it were a child? Once we'd covered every angle, I still wasn't completely settled on a decision. But instead of dumping my lingering anxiety on my agent who had other things to do, I asked if there was anywhere to go to think and be alone. She sent me to an empty office down the hall.

I was tempted to make cell phone calls and get more noise going, but something tugged at me to just be quiet. I sat in some employee's office in complete stillness. I breathed and breathed and the noise faded away. It became a meditation. I just sat and savored the silence, just let my heart and head rest. Then I prayed for clarity and peace. I asked God to lead me to the right place and let me know by the peace I would feel in my soul.

After half an hour, I felt total calm. When I went back to Linda's office, I asked if she thought accepting the offer was the right choice. She did. The peace in me confirmed it. She accepted the offer over the phone, then we let out a cheer.

It turned out that while I was meditating, the publishing industry was imploding. That day in December 2008 was called Black Wednesday in the publishing business. Random House announced a massive restructuring. Simon & Schuster cut 35 jobs. Thomas Nelson laid off 10 percent of its staff. On one of the worst days for the publishing industry, somehow I got a book deal.

It was mind-blowing.

It was nearing 5 p.m. and I needed to hop a cab to return to my sister's before it became impossible to get home. The masses were heading to the lighting of the Christmas tree at

Rockefeller Center. I didn't know my way around the city and wasn't sure of the best spot to hail a cab. Somehow, I found one right away. I climbed inside and we slid into the traffic jam of noisy horns. It took 15 minutes to go one block. For a minute, I started to worry about how much the ride would cost, then I started to laugh. I just got a book deal. I could afford a long cab ride.

I was tempted to call everyone I knew to celebrate, but I wanted to just sit and give thanks for a moment. It was then that the silence completely enveloped me, as if I'd been wrapped in a blanket of peace. The cab ride felt holy as a chapel. I felt a sense of oneness with God, a completion of sorts, as if I were surrounded both inside and outside with a peace that truly surpassed all understanding.

Something in me said, *Remember this moment. This is your sign that all is well. Don't ever doubt this deal, this book.*

How do you get moments of great peace?

You practice being open to them daily.

I once heard of a woman who took a day every week to be completely silent. That might seem extreme, but imagine how quiet it must be in her head. I've learned to pause throughout the day and be quiet. My friends in recovery taught me the simplicity of the Serenity Prayer. Whenever you find yourself lost in confusion, doubt, or indecision, you simply pause, quiet the noise, and in the stillness say, "God, grant me the serenity to accept the things I cannot change, courage to change the things I can, and wisdom to know the difference."

I practice being quiet every day. It's like an ATM. You can't take money out of that machine unless you have put money in the bank. If you make frequent deposits, when you need money, it's there. I spend the first 30 minutes of the day alone with God. I invest daily in peace and quiet. Every morning, God gets the first half hour. It's the most valuable time of the day. It's the most important thing I do. I check in with my Source of love, creativity, inspiration, and beauty. I plug into my power source.

It will transform your life if you commit to it daily. Nothing usually happens during that half hour. I just sit in God's presence, and, somehow, later in the day, when I need it most, peace will come to me.

I've discovered that the best way to turn down the noise is to turn up the quiet.

To be a channel of peace,
you have to stay open.

One day two strangers wandered down our driveway. Two kids, on the verge of becoming teenagers, kids I'd never seen in the neighborhood. One of them yanked one of our snowplow poles out of the ground and started to wander into our backyard.

I watched from upstairs, worried they would steal something. I expected the worst simply because I didn't know them. Were they staking out houses to rob? Were they going to smash a window with the pole?

Before I could decide what to do, my husband walked outside and greeted them with, "Hey, guys, how you doing? We need that for the snowplow, so you're going to have to put that back."

He chatted with them, they put the stake back, then climbed over a neighbor's fence to take a shortcut home. I watched until they were out of sight, still uncertain of their motives.

All day I felt guilty for assuming the worst in them. As a kid, I cut through yards to take a shorter route home. So did my daughter. We used to laugh at the elderly neighbor on our street who cut through everyone's yard to get home but went ballistic whenever kids cut through her yard.

Another time I assumed the worst one day at a drugstore when I saw a cluster of boys in droopy pants whispering and giggling in a huddle. My first thought? Shoplifters.

My husband, who looks for the best in everyone, struck up a conversation. He learned where they went to school and how their grades were.

When I got to the cash register, I was short 25 cents. I yelled to my husband for it. He didn't hear me, but one of the boys did. The boy came over, dug in his pocket, and handed me a quarter. "Here, Miss," he said.

My heart melted.

Why do I sometimes assume the worst from strangers? I question their behavior, but I should question mine. I close off my heart and think it makes me safer somehow.

I wonder if the hearts of others close up when I talk too much or too loudly or drop an F bomb now and then or sprinkle in sarcastic remarks to be witty. Do they close when I play my country music too loud or use my car horn to say hello and good-bye to family and friends?

George Bernard Shaw wrote that the great secret wasn't about having good or bad manners, but having the same kind of manners for everyone. What would happen if we expected everyone to turn out to be good, not bad? What would the world look like or feel like if we kept our hearts open to everyone?

I grew up singing the Saint Francis prayer hymn, "Make Me a Channel of Your Peace," at church on Sundays. But I never knew how to actually be that channel. I repeat that prayer every morning as my mission statement, but I got new clarity on it when my sister Joan sent me a copy of the book *The Untethered Soul* by Michael Singer.

He wrote that we all build up lives that buffer us from hurt and from each other, and ultimately from life itself. We close ourselves off from others to protect ourselves, but in the end, it doesn't make us free, we become a prisoner to our fears. We lock inside ourselves a scared person who doesn't get to grow up.

How do you stay open? Michael Singer says the secret is to stop closing. Too many of us suffer from heart blockages caused by fear. Writer Emmet Fox compared that open spiritual channel to a water hose. When you water the lawn with the hose, there's an endless source of water that flows through the hose unless something is blocking the water. Step on the hose or bend it, and the water stops. The water, the source, is still there, but the channel is blocked so nothing gets out.

I spent most of my adult life protecting myself from getting hurt. I was a pro at closing, but found the world is full of possibilities when you stay open. It becomes a more magical place. Let me tell you about one winter night when one woman opened her heart and set off a chain reaction.

I had planned to go to the Cleveland International Film Festival with my husband that March, but most of the roads were closed. The snow had piled up so high, hardly anyone ventured out. We knew the car wouldn't even make it out of the driveway. And if it did, AAA wasn't going to rescue us. There wouldn't be a tow truck available on a night like this. Only a fool would be driving. Or so I thought.

My husband agreed, but a few hours later announced, "Let's go out to eat. We'll walk." Walk? My husband walk? I was tempted to feel his forehead. He did have a fever—cabin fever. Spending a Saturday night at home was too much for this extrovert.

He climbed into a coat that looks like a comforter with arms. Nanook of the North had to look in the mirror to figure out how to close all the snaps, zippers, and Velcro contraptions.

We trudged down the sidewalk and hiked in slow motion to Nighttown, a jazz club and restaurant half a mile away. It was dark out and the streets were deserted. A few ghostly figures walked in the road. We saw no cars.

We thawed while we ate at the restaurant. We chatted with the staff, then left. I wanted to hoof it and get home as fast as possible. It was uphill going home and my frozen jeans had thawed during dinner and were soaked.

Through the snowy haze, we saw three sets of taillights glowing like red eyes. An SUV and a van stopped to help a car stuck on the hill. The car couldn't grip the snow and kept sliding down. *What fool drove tonight?* I wondered.

An old woman unrolled her window. I tried to help her steer, but the Cadillac had no traction. It spun out every two feet. She would never make it up the hill. She was headed for home, about ten miles away. What was she doing out in this mess?

"I worked at the Cleveland Clinic all day," she said. "I'm a nurse."

A nurse? Oh, my. We had to get her home. I looked at the hill. Even if she got up the hill, what if she got stuck on the drive home? There would be no one to help her. My heart sank.

The man in the SUV took out a long strap. He wanted to pull her car up the hill but couldn't attach the strap. The lady in the van took charge. She told us her name was Angela, then ordered the nurse to scoot over and took the wheel. Angela hollered to my husband to get into her van and push the car up the hill. I wasn't sure what to do, so I climbed into the backseat of the car.

The van bumped gently into the car, over and over, until it crawled up the hill. Instead of stopping at the top to let us out to walk home, Angela kept driving. My husband followed. He had no idea whose van he was driving or where she was going. Neither did I.

Loretta, the nurse, told me she was 75 and had been a nurse for 51 years. "If I retired, I might just forget to get out of bed in the morning," she said.

Angela's van was full of bundles of the *New York Times* that she had been delivering to stores. She never said it, but this detour taking Loretta home would make her late and disrupt her evening. Angela smiled and chatted as if there were nothing in the world she would rather be doing.

Our little convoy crawled up the hill and on and on, all the way to Loretta's home ten miles away. It took more than an hour to get there. Loretta tried to give us each a twenty. We tossed the money back at her. She was grateful and so were we—grateful for people like her, who showed up at work to care for strangers on a day when it would have been easier to call it off.

We all waved good-bye to her, then my husband and I climbed into the back of the van, way in the back behind stacks of newspapers, and laughed as a perfect stranger drove us home.

God will not have His work made manifest by cowards.

I keep a pink Post-it note stuck to the computer where I write my columns and books: "God will not have His work made manifest by cowards." It jump-starts me out of paralyzing fear and into my work. The quote from Ralph Waldo Emerson is like Uncle Sam's finger pointing at me in the military recruiting poster.

It's my version of the saying "Feel the fear and do it anyway."

A friend once told me, "I was good at water-skiing because I was afraid of the water." While fear keeps many from taking action, it can actually be a great motivator. It doesn't have to stop you. It can propel you forward. Sometimes I grab its hand and say, "Come on, fear, let's get moving." I treat fear like a companion I'm stuck with, but we don't stay stuck. I drag fear along with me as I write. Action is a great antidote to fear.

Too many of us feel fear, then hit the brakes. The ad campaign "Don't Almost Give. Give" is so powerful because we see ourselves in it. Too often we're so close to helping someone, but fear trumps our compassion. We talk ourselves out of being useful or generous or thoughtful or powerful. But you can't change the world by hoping somebody else will take action.

So how do you move from fear to action? Sometimes you take baby steps; sometimes you take one giant leap. Sometimes faith will come along and fear flees. But often faith and fear walk hand in hand for a while.

My friends in recovery who attend Alcoholics Anonymous meetings taught me to list my fears, put them down in black and white, and face them once and for all. The next step is to share the list with someone trustworthy and get down to the causes and conditions of each one. Then pray for the fears to be removed.

I try to practice the opposite of fear. My fear muscle is way overdeveloped. My faith muscle looks like the arm of a wimp. I have to give it a workout, and practice believing in that wonderful quote, "The will of God will never lead you where the grace of God cannot keep you."

I'm constantly inspired by the people I meet who find the courage to change the things they can, sometimes against all odds.

I got to know Melinda Elkins after her mother was murdered. Someone had raped and beaten her mother and also raped and beaten Melinda's niece, who survived the attack. The little girl had been spending the night at her grandma's house in Barberton, Ohio.

The police arrested Melinda's husband, Clarence, for the murder. A jury convicted him based on the testimony of the six-year-old niece, who gave conflicting accounts of what she saw in the dark. There was never any physical evidence to link Clarence to the crime. Prosecutors built an entire murder case on the traumatized niece, who later recanted her testimony.

Melinda's life turned upside down. She was grieving for her mother when she also lost her husband to prison. She believed in his innocence when no one else did. In the seven years he spent in prison, she used her power to keep pestering attorneys, judges, and police to reopen and reinvestigate the case. Meanwhile, she lost her home as she struggled as a single parent to their two sons. She had no criminal justice experience, just passion for the truth and the power of the promise she made to her mom to find the real killer.

Melinda examined every aspect of the case. It troubled her that, when her little niece woke up after the crime, she had gone next door for help but the neighbor lady never called the police. That woman made the girl wait outside the door while she gathered her purse then drove the girl home. Melinda never understood why that neighbor refused to call the police or let the girl in. That question led her to investigate the woman's boyfriend, Earl Mann. He had been staying with the woman and their three daughters. By the time Melinda found that information out, Earl was in prison for abusing his children. As fate would have it, Earl was in the same prison as Clarence. One day Earl dropped a cigarette and Clarence grabbed it. He sent it home and Melinda urged her attorneys to have the DNA tested. Earl's DNA matched the DNA left at the crime scene.

Melinda's husband walked out of prison a free man after seven years.

Another man walked out of prison after 20 years on death row after a priest summoned the faith to speak up for him. Father Neil Kakoothe visits men on Ohio's death row to offer spiritual counsel. He knows he can't single-handedly end the death penalty, but the Roman Catholic priest did just that for one man. When he discovered Joe D'Ambrosio might be innocent, Father Neil took home boxes of files and investigated the case.

He found so many flaws in the case that sent Joe to prison, the courts granted the inmate a new trial. It turned out that, in the original trial, the prosecutors had hidden ten pieces of key evidence, information that the jury never saw that most likely would have led to a not-guilty verdict.

Joe needed a place to live while he was awaiting the new trial. He had nowhere to go. While he was in prison, he lost his family. A widow and grandmother of four who barely knew him opened up her home. Rosalie Lee had befriended Joe after her daughter met him through a friend years before Joe was convicted of murder.

For years, Rosalie drove to a maximum-security prison to visit Joe. He had few visitors. His parents had died and his two sisters lived in Florida. For 20 years, Joe called her Mom. On his birthdays, she bought a vending machine cupcake and stuck tiny pretzel sticks in—he wasn't allowed candles.

"He's the son I never had," she told me. Her husband, also named Joe, died. When she visited the cemetery on holidays, she set flowers on his grave and on Joe's parents' graves.

The judge allowed Joe to move in with Rosalie while he

awaited a new trial. Rosalie set up a small bedroom for Joe with a TV, phone, and stereo. Rosalie had to give up her caller ID and call waiting so the phone could accommodate Joe's electronic monitoring device.

Months later, a judge ruled that no new trial was needed. Joe D'Ambrosio was a free man. Father Neil called Rosalie a blessing. "She not only hears the Gospel," he said. "She lives it."

It takes special courage to reach out to the people the world would rather write off.

"I'm only trying to be a good Christian," Rosalie said.

That takes true bravery.

Leave a legacy time can't erase.

It's amazing how much you learn about someone at their funeral.

Funerals have a way of making you take stock of your own life, examine where you've traveled, where you're headed, and what you'll leave behind when the journey is over.

When my friend Margi's husband died, I learned that this quiet man had a laugh that was so hearty and loud no one forgot it. Greg Lofaro worked in the counseling program at Kent State University where they created audiotapes for training. At the funeral, they told how they usually reused the tapes but because Greg's laughter was so loud, they couldn't erase it off the tapes.

On a retreat once, a woman told how she was at a funeral when a nine-year-old delivered part of the eulogy. Everyone held their breath as the little girl approached the microphone.

"Grandma wore lipstick and drove with the top down," the girl said. That was it. What a great way to describe Grandma's zest for life.

When my uncle Jack died at 76, his son Mike gave the eulogy. Uncle Jack was the soft-spoken, gentle uncle who didn't pester you about what you were going to do with your life after college or why you were 30 and still single. I never realized how little I knew about him until his funeral.

I learned my uncle grew up during the Depression and never had money to go to college. He insisted his four children go. They joked that their first words as toddlers were, "Go to college." They all did.

I learned that my uncle was a math whiz whose title was Director of Financial Forecasting at TRW. He was audited by the IRS once because the government couldn't believe a man with three sons in college would really give that much money to charity.

Uncle Jack retired after 43 years with the same company, but his work history was barely mentioned. His worth was measured by the grandchildren who gathered at a microphone and sang to him, "Did you ever know that you're my hero?" His worth was measured by the "son" he took in when his own kids were teens. The boy had lost both parents, so Uncle Jack and Aunt Kate raised him as their own.

His worth was measured by the size of his heart, not the estate he left behind.

Too often we get caught up measuring our daily lives by how we look, perform, or impress others with our achievements. We set five-year goals to increase our income, build our portfolios, strengthen our 401(k)s. We think we're a success when we buy a faster car, bigger house, or obtain another college degree.

The measure of my uncle's worth was summed up in three things: his faith, his family, and his contributions to others. His granddaughter read a passage from Ray Bradbury's book *Fahrenheit 451*, about how years after your grandfather is gone, if you could peer inside your skull you'd find the imprint where he touched you.

You leave a legacy time can't erase by touching people deeply.

So what will they say at your funeral? What stories will they tell long after it's over? What legacy will you leave?

Some people suggest writing your own epitaph, eulogy, or obituary, then living up to it. Reading your obit can change your life. It did for Alfred Nobel, who was known in his time for his invention of dynamite. When his brother died, the newspaper confused the two men and published Alfred's obituary instead of his brother's. It read: "Dr. Alfred Nobel, who became rich by finding ways to kill more people faster than ever before, died yesterday."

When he read his own obituary, Alfred realized he was going to be remembered for creating something that destroyed lives. He created and funded the Nobel Prizes, setting aside the bulk of his estate—a $9 million endowment fund—to establish the awards. They're given every year for achievements in everything from physical science to peace. His name is now connected to celebrating humankind's greatest achievements.

You don't have to create or win the Nobel Prize to be remembered long after you're gone.

Andy Berry was a camp ranger at Camp Manatoc in Ohio. They called him the Keeper. He made sure your tent didn't have a hole, your cabin roof didn't leak, your canoe didn't take in water. He taught thousands of boys how to handle an ax, sharpen a penknife, build a fire, and put it out to preserve the forest for others.

He worked every weekend for 25 years at Boy Scout camp. His smile never faded, not even when a boy would sneak in a gas lantern, poke a hole in a tent, or forget to clean a cabin. He was a second dad to boys who had no one to show them how to check the oil in a car, repair a lawn mower, or fix a broken pipe. His goal was to make sure every Scout had a great time without getting hurt. He'd been raised on a farm and had to quit school in the eighth grade to work and support the family. He made sure other boys had all the opportunities he never got.

Alice Hamill Hartman taught school in tiny Minerva, Ohio. She was no fragile old soul, even though she was a tiny thing with glasses and messy hair. She'd run through the halls laughing and pause to dance a little jig. On her eighty-fifth birthday, when she was substituting for a fifth-grade teacher, she decided to buy birthday treats for all the students and walked 20 blocks to the store. When she died at 99, the first thing the obituary mentioned was how Alice broke her leg in her eighties when she fell out of an apple tree. She taught everyone to celebrate life.

Henry Luckhardt grew up in the hollers of West Virginia. He was just five when his sister Rose pulled a pot of boiling water off the stove and scalded herself. She was seven when she died as a result of the burns. Henry worked in the coal mines, then moved to Akron, joined the army where he earned bronze stars at Normandy, Ardennes, and the Rhineland. He built a modest home and worked at a tire plant until he retired in 1962. He was a small-town man who never spent a dime on himself. He wore 30-year-old shirts and pants with patches on the knees. He spent just $15 on groceries every week. He drove a '72 Oldsmobile that lasted him until 1999 when he died at 91. It had only 20,000 miles on it.

It shocked everyone when he died and left $1.4 million to the burn center at Akron Children's Hospital. The man who seemed to have so little had invested it all so he could leave a fortune to save little girls like Rose.

Then there was Randy Stang, who gave the speech of his life at city hall one night in his hometown, Bay Village, Ohio. Others came to complain about the proposed skateboard and bike park. Don't build it near my backyard, they said. Randy gave a passionate plea for the park, telling them all he lived next to the park and didn't mind the noise and lights from the basketball courts, or the stray Frisbees, golf balls, and baseballs that landed in his yard.

"I'm in favor of a skate and bike park," he told them all. "I am wondering if the citizens against the park have no grandchildren, no children, or are not a child themselves."

He welcomed the bike and skating park and invited the city to build it near his house. "You want to put it just to the north of that baseball diamond there, probably about 50 feet from my yard."

Then he fell silent. As soon as he finished speaking, he collapsed. A doctor and nurse tried to revive him. Randy Stang was 55. He left behind a wife and four children. And he left us all with a legacy, with new words to live by.

We constantly hear people vow all the time, almost threaten, "Not in my backyard." Perhaps you've said it. I confess that I have. Randy's message? I believe so much in my community and in other people's children, put that park in my backyard. When the people of Bay Village approved the skating park, they named it after Randy.

I love the advice Saint Francis of Assisi gave his followers:

> Keep a clear eye toward life's end. Do not forget your purpose and destiny as God's creature. What you are in His sight is what you are and nothing more.
>
> Do not let worldly cares and anxieties or the pressures of office blot out the divine life within you or the voice of God's Spirit guiding your great task of leading humanity to wholeness. If you open yourself to God and His plan printed deeply in your heart, God will open Himself to you. Remember that when you leave this earth, you can take with you nothing that you have received—fading symbols of honor, trappings of power,—but only what you have given: a full heart enriched by honest service, love, sacrifice and courage.

That's how you outlive your life. You live a legacy time can't erase, because you leave it in the hearts of others.

If you woke up today,
God isn't through with you yet.

How many people does it take to change the world?

One.

It doesn't matter how much money you have or how much time you have left or how much energy you have. You're never too old or too sick or too broke or too broken to be of use to God. It's been said that man's finish is God's beginning. When I was feeling my worst after chemotherapy and daily radiation treatments, every morning these words inspired me to get out of bed and climb into life:

If you woke up today, God isn't through with you yet.

I glued those words to my morning meditation book after seeing them in a newspaper article. You aren't finished until God says you are. If you're still here, there's a reason.

Maybe more than one.

My friends in recovery attend the annual Founders Day

weekend of Alcoholics Anonymous every year in June. The fellowship started in Akron, Ohio.

Three portraits sit on easels in front of the stage where thousands gather from around the world to honor the founders of AA. There's a giant black-and-white photo of Bill Wilson, who failed miserably as a stockbroker. There's a poster-size picture of Dr. Robert Smith, whose hands used to shake during surgery from too much whiskey. There's a huge picture of Sister Mary Ignatia, who was a music teacher until she had a mental breakdown. She was stripped of her duties and sent to do something harmless like run the flower room at a local hospital. She ended up helping Dr. Bob treat drunks as patients; they saw alcoholics in a new light, as people with a disease called alcoholism that could actually be treated.

When all three of them hit rock bottom, that's when they were called to ascend to something greater than they ever imagined. Together, they helped launch a spiritual fellowship that has saved millions of lives. Our failure can actually be God's starting point. You aren't finished until God says you are. You might be through, but God might just be getting started.

Don't ever give up on yourself, on what you alone can offer the world. As long as you're on the right side of the grass, you're still needed in this world.

I met Ella Mae Cheeks Johnson when she was 101. She had traveled to 30 countries and outlived two husbands. Ella Mae dug through a stack of papers and pulled out the speech she wrote when she turned 90. Nope, not that one. She grabbed the speech she wrote when she turned 95. Nope, wrong again. She pulled out the speech she gave when she turned 100.

Her black wheelchair barely contained her energy. She scooted her feet across the floor to navigate it to the bookshelves. She had just finished reading *Confessions of an Economic Hit Man*.

I met her in 2005, shortly after she received the Distinguished Alumni Award from the Mandel School of Applied Social Sciences at Case Western Reserve University. At the time, she was the oldest living graduate of the program. When a dean went to visit her, she was reading the 9/11 Commission report.

"I wanted to know what they found out," she told me.

At her hundredth-birthday party, she printed a list of her favorite books and passed it out to guests. A picture of the Good Samaritan she painted 81 years earlier sat on her dresser. The Bible story about the man who stopped to help a beaten stranger others had ignored had shaped her whole life.

Her first good Samaritans were her neighbors, Mr. and Mrs. Davis. They became her parents the day her mom died, when she was four. She got a college degree in French, but a black woman wasn't allowed to teach French, so she became a social worker.

She moved to Cleveland and got her master's degree in 1928. She worked for the county welfare department and once helped a client named Louise Stokes, whose son, Louis, went on to become a congressman, and whose brother, Carl, became the first black mayor of a major city.

That painting is the last thing she sees before she falls asleep and the first thing she sees when she wakes. It is the challenge by which Ella Mae Johnson lives. It is her version of "Yes, we can."

When she turned 105, she traveled to Washington, D.C., to witness the inauguration of the first black president. Ella Mae died in 2010, right before her memoir, *It Is Well with My Soul: The Extraordinary Life of a 106-Year-Old Woman*, was published. In all her years, she never had a master plan. She led the Master plan.

Evelyn Boyd has earned the right to sit around and do nothing. When I met her she was 92 and had spent 33 years teaching music, most of them in the Cleveland public schools. It always bothered her that some students in grade school couldn't read the words to the songs she taught.

She could isolate herself as a lonely widow on a pension and cling to every dime. Instead, she volunteers at the Cleveland Clinic and at the Society for the Blind. She spends $30 a pop to buy books for children she will never meet.

Every time the Daedalus Books catalog arrives, she studies the synopsis of each book and orders the best ones. She has the books delivered directly to a pediatrician for his Reach Out and Read program. She has donated more than 500 new books.

Dr. Robert Needlman started the program after he noticed that the medical center waiting room in the inner city of Boston had no books for the children to read while they waited. The staff noticed the children stealing the books, so they stopped putting books out. The fact that children wanted to read so badly inspired Needlman to raise money to buy thousands of books to give away to every child with every checkup.

Then he recruited volunteers to read aloud to children in the waiting room. That's how he and Barry Zuckerman started the national nonprofit Reach Out and Read more than 20 years ago. They wanted to see every child grow up with the chance to love books. So did Evelyn.

"I had a good life," she said. "I didn't have it by myself. We didn't come into this world just for ourselves. We're here to help others."

We're here to live a life for others. The Jesuits taught me to build my life upon the principle and foundation that Saint Ignatius of Loyola taught: To know, love, and serve God and be happy with God forever. Everything here is a gift created for us to experience God more fully. We are to keep those gifts if they enhance our growth or release those gifts if they diminish our growth.

Saint Ignatius went on to say we are to remain indifferent and unattached to everything if we don't have clarity about what is the best choice. We aren't to prefer health over sickness, a long life over a short one, wealth over poverty. We serve God wherever we find ourselves, sick or well, young or old, rich or poor. We are to desire only that which enhances our spiritual growth, which could be anything.

Cancer taught me to love life no matter what the circumstances. It's a scary disease, but it comes with its own gifts. Cancer rubs your nose into life. Every so often someone still asks, "So, are you in remission?" They really want to know if I'm cured. My prognosis is the same as anyone who's ever had cancer and it's the same as anyone who has never had cancer.

We get to live all the days of our lives.

It's up to us, not cancer, or any other disease or disability or disappointment in life. Most people with cancer aren't dying from cancer. They don't get the diagnosis, go home, crawl into bed, and wait to die. They are living with it. They are living past it. They are living in spite of it. They go to work. They raise children. They go fishing. They make love. They plant gardens.

For years a lovely woman in my newsroom came to work every day with terminal cancer. You couldn't tell Arlene Flynn had anything wrong with her. Her hair was perfectly coifed, her makeup flawless, her smile wider than anyone's. She didn't look like a dying woman.

When I found out she had cancer and tried to console her, she only smiled and told me about all the interesting people she had met that week getting chemo. She made it sound like a party.

Arlene squeezed so much life out of her life, at her funeral I had a hard time believing that she was really gone.

But we all have a shelf life. We're all going to expire. No one, not even the best doctor, possesses a magic slide rule that calculates the day you'll die right down to the hour. Doctors gave my dad six months. He only had weeks. Doctors gave a woman I met one year. She's still kicking after ten.

No one knows the hour death will call, not even those who have been diagnosed with cancer.

We just know to make all the hours of living worthwhile.

Acknowledgments

To write a book, you have to silence the voices inside that scream that you can't or whisper that you shouldn't or taunt that you won't ever finish.

I am eternally grateful for...

All the family and friends who made their voices louder than all the doubt inside me. Your endless support and love are priceless.

My husband, Bruce Hennes, who doesn't mind sleeping alone when inspiration keeps me up till 3 a.m. The depth of your love still blows me away.

My daughter, Gabrielle, my first miracle. Thanks for all the love and laughter we share every single day.

My sons, Ben, Joe, and James, for your love and light, and for sharing your computer, photography, and social media expertise.

My grandson, Asher, for being my joy, and Baby Boo-ba-loo, who arrives soon.

All who bought and read my first book, *God Never Blinks: 50 Lessons for Life's Little Detours*. Countless writers who offered their support, especially Dr. Michael Roizen, Joe Eszterhas, Jeffrey Zaslow, Dick Feagler, Thrity Umrigar, Dan Chaon, and Deepak Chopra.

My colleagues at the *Plain Dealer*, especially Barb Galbincea, Chris Quinn, Thom Fladung, Debra Adam Simmons, Shirley Stineman, Susan Goldberg, and Terry Egger, for giving me the freedom to do my best work and for granting me permission to share it in this book.

All those who allowed me to share their stories in my columns and in this book. You will never know how many lives you have transformed.

The dear friends who inspire me and keep me centered, especially Sheryl Harris, Vicki Prussak, and Beth Welch.

The sources of inspiration at the Carmelite monastery, the Jesuit Retreat House, and The Gathering Place.

My agent and the awesome team at Grand Central Publishing. Thanks for believing in both books and for reaching so high we hit the top: *New York Times* best seller. WOW! I'm still blown away by all of you.

Linda Loewenthal, my agent at David Black Literary Agency. What a rare gem you are. Thanks for guiding me with your wisdom, your patience, and your enthusiasm. You were right. *This* was the next book to write!

Publisher Jamie Raab: Your enthusiasm should be bottled and sold. Editor Karen Murgolo: Only you can make being edited feel so, so good.

Carolyn Kurek, for putting out fires big and small; Matthew Ballast, Jennifer Musico, and Dana Trombley, for spreading the word about the book so far (I'm still getting e-mails from Brazil, Australia, and China); Philippa White, who does more to help me than I'll ever know; Diane Luger, who designs covers that look like gifts; Nicole Bond, for getting the book into 18 countries; Peggy Boelke, who spread it over all 50 states; and thanks to all those in sales and marketing, for spreading my message of hope.

The bookstores big and small, and all the libraries in tiny towns like Ravenna, Ohio, where I grew up. Thanks for sharing the joy of reading.

And as always, endless gratitude to the Source of it all, the God of my joy.

About the Author

REGINA BRETT is author of the *New York Times* bestseller *God Never Blinks: 50 Lessons for Life's Little Detours* and is a columnist for the *Plain Dealer* in Cleveland, Ohio. She has twice been named a finalist for the Pulitzer Prize in Commentary and has received numerous writing awards, including the National Headliner Award for her columns on breast cancer in 1999 and in 2009. Brett also hosts her own call-in radio show, *The Regina Brett Show*, on WKSU, northeast Ohio's National Public Radio affiliate.

She lives in Cleveland, Ohio, with her husband, Bruce.

Her website is www.reginabrett.com.